THE
HEALNG
POTENTIAL
OF
TM

The Healing Potential of Transcendental Meditation

DR. UNA KROLL

JOHN KNOX PRESS
ATLANTA,

Library of Congress Cataloging in Publication Data

Kroll, Una.
    The healing potential of transcendental meditation.

    Bibliography: p.
    1. Transcendental meditation. I. Title.
[DNLM: 1. Religion and psychology. 2. Thinking.
BL627 K929h]
BL627.K76   1974b   294.5'43   74-7615
ISBN 0-8042-0598-1

First published in Great Britain in 1974 by
Darton, Longman & Todd, Ltd
85 Gloucester Road, London, SW7 4SU
Published in the United States of America by
John Knox Press, Atlanta, Georgia 1974
Printed in the United States of America

Second Printing 1976

Contents

For my own guru, my husband

Acknowledgement

I am grateful to Maharishi Mahesh Yogi for permission to make quotations from his works. I am also grateful to Professor Dorothy Emmet and the Epiphany Philosophers at Cambridge who enabled me to have an interesting discussion with Dr A. Campbell and Mr John Windsor which clarified my thoughts on several points. The discussion first appeared in *Theoria to theory* and is reprinted by kind permission of the editor.

Introduction

Last year John came to see me in surgery. His death sentence was already obvious in his X-rays. He told me that he had smoked heavily all his life because it calmed his nerves in his very demanding responsible job. 'If I didn't smoke', he said, 'I'd lose my temper all the time. Anyway, doctor, you remember the time I did give it up after you'd lectured me. I grew as fat as a pig and that wasn't any good for my heart, was it?' John is one of the many victims of the pressures of modern urban living. Many stresses will have contributed to his death. Human beings like John react to stressful situations in their lives in different ways. A delicate balance exists between every individual and his environment. Some react to stress efficiently and appropriately, especially when they are young or the stress is short lived. Others are destroyed by complex events in their lives over which they have only partial control. It is known that stress contributes to diseases such as cancer of the lung, high blood pressure, coronary thrombosis and chronic bronchitis. It is frightening to see the increasing number of young men who die from heart attacks each year. Unresolved emotional distress can alter the balance of a man's sanity and cause him to commit suicide.

Stress can be beneficial, of course. For instance, the

challenge of competition makes men and women seek perfection in love, work and sport. However, there are many times when the body over-reacts to stress. This over-reaction may become habitual. In time irreversible changes take place. When that happens the body is subject to wear and tear of its own making. This self-destructive process, if continued for many months and years, may result either in physical disease or psychological illness.

It is evident that any way of lessening stress will benefit society. Progress is being made towards reducing pollution, noise levels, overcrowding in big cities and long working hours. A different approach to the problem of stress is to protect the individual from its effects. Noise can be kept out by using ear plugs. People can move from town into the country. Sometimes, however, the defences are inadequate and stress begins to take its toll of the body. Even at that stage there are ways of overcoming it. Drugs, psychotherapy, relaxation techniques, such as yoga, have been used to combat stress. One of the more recent ways of overcoming stress within the body is offered by the technique known as Transcendental Meditation, or TM.

On the last day of 1957 Transcendental Meditation was introduced into Western society by Maharishi Mahesh Yogi. He had developed a technique of deep relaxation by which the mind was taken to the source of thought, the pure field of creative intelligence. He claimed that in this way the conscious mind was expanded, its power increased and the body gained more energy. Man could in this way make use of his full mental potential. His teaching was taken up enthusiastically, and in

America students began to meditate in large numbers. Some of the physical effects of the technique were quickly apparent. University scientists began systematic studies of the physiological and psychological effects of meditation and by 1970 there was already a lot of documented evidence about TM. Distinctive changes in the brain wave rhythms during meditation were described. Physiological changes were recorded under laboratory conditions. Meditators reported a cumulative growth in calmness, alertness and efficiency and they said that their sense of well-being persisted for some time beyond the immediate post-meditation period. Some people noted a decreased craving for drugs like alchohol and tobacco. Reports appeared about people who had been cured of their addiction to 'hard' drugs through the regular practice of Transcendental Meditation.

These scientific reports had to be taken seriously. When the Maharishi had begun teaching his method to the Western world in 1957 he had burst on to the television screens at a time when the media were fascinated by the 'third world'. Esoteric movements were given publicity, some of which was laudatory. Much of the publicity was hostile and focused on the personalities of those people who learnt to meditate. Among these were the Beatles who departed with the Guru to Rishikesh when they were at the height of their popularity. The fact that TM was simple but had to be taught individually for a fee of a week's wages wrapped the technique in some mystery.

In 1957 there were few guidelines to help the bystander to know whether the Maharishi was a true or a false prophet. The Western world was already trying to assimilate many new ideas about the life styles of some twentieth century Christians like the 'Jesus freaks' and the Neopentecostalists. In the Christian mind meditation was equated with prayer. At the same time there was a resurgence of interest in techniques like Yoga and Zen meditation. The teachings of this new guru spread rapidly in America and more than a quarter of a million people have learnt the technique since its introduction. In Great Britain the number of meditators have increased more slowly but steadily and twenty thousand people have been taught to meditate Maharishi style. Little is yet known about the personalities of the people who take up meditation or about their motivation. One of the major claims for TM is that the physiological effects of stress are minimised by the deep relaxation of the body during meditation. This claim has been scientifically substantiated and so there seems to be good reason for thoughtful people to learn more about the Maharishi Mahesh Yogi and his ideas and method.

Some of the scientific experiments on volunteer meditators were published in England in medical journals and it was because of this that I became interested in TM. As a Christian family doctor I have been alarmed by the rising incidence of stress disease in this country. I know that many people who come to me are suffering from the effects of stress in their lives. People now consult their doctors quite freely about domestic disharmony, personal and sexual inadequacy, conflicts at work, advertising pressures and anxieties of many kinds. They come to see their doctor before they are overtly ill and seek relief. Unfortunately their doctor is also pressurised for time and energy. The present resources of the National Health Service are inadequate to provide more than a first-aid service for the victims of social diseases although it does provide a good break-down service for those who have been defeated by the demands of modern life, once they have become ill. The family doctor's response to people suffering from stress varies. Sometimes there is time to sit down and listen so that the patient can sort out the various priorities in life and find ways of reducing stress or of coping with it more efficiently. Sometimes scarcity of time, the severity of the stress or the personality of the patient compel the doctor to use tranquillizers or anti-depressant drugs. Often the only real help to the patient comes in the shape of a blunt warning to the patient coupled with sufficient time off work to allow his natural resources to recuperate. The problem is now so large that I have become increasingly aware of the need to find ways in which people can be helped to preserve their health and to enjoy their lives. In this context Transcendental Meditation seemed to have real potential. It offered a simple and enjoyable method of achieving deep relaxation with subsequent improvement in energy.

It is because of a real need among my patients that I set out to study both the Maharishi Mahesh Yogi and his method. When I began this study I had two main objectives: as a doctor I wanted to make sure that patients could not be harmed by TM; as a Christian I wanted to see how the technique related to prayer.

'The fruit of the Spirit is love, joy, peace, patience, kindness, goodness, faithfulness, gentleness, self-control : against such there is no law.'

Galatians : 5 : 22–23.

'The faith of a man follows his nature,
    Arunja.
Man is made of faith : as his faith is,
    so is he.'

Bhagavad Gita : 17 : 3.

1 The guru

I am glad that I have never met the Maharishi Mahesh Yogi in person. It has enabled me to see his teaching in a more objective way than otherwise would have been possible. Every teacher uses his personality to communicate his message. The initial impact of any spoken teaching depends largely upon the non-verbal communication which takes place between the teacher and his audience. It is easy to be fascinated or repelled by the appearance, personality and mannerisms of a teacher. Either of these immediate emotive reactions can lastingly affect a student's perceptions and colour his judgement. My initial contact with the Maharishi was through his books. Subsequently, like millions of other people, I caught a glimpse of him on television, read about him in the newspapers. Later I heard about him from his close disciples.

What a man is, is reflected in many different ways. What a man does, is on permanent record. What a man leaves behind him after death is his teaching and the enthusiasm of his immediate disciples who continue to develop his ideas. The Maharishi is still alive. The importance of all his teachings cannot yet be fully assessed because they have not been put to the test of time. His method of Transcendental Meditation, however, is not

B

new. There is evidence that it was known as long ago as five hundred years before Christ, at the time the Bhagavad Gita was written. The Maharishi says that he was personally instructed in the method by his own teacher, Swami Brahamananda Saraswati (1869–1953). It is on the value of the method, which he has introduced all over the world, that the Maharishi will be assessed in the future.

The Maharishi was born at Jubblepore, Central India, about sixty-one years ago. He is a reticent man who speaks little about himself and never about his early years. He is steeped in Hindu culture. It is likely that as a child he would have known the great strength of the Hindu extended family system where several generations live together under one roof. The younger children pay great respect to their elders and there is always a sense of cohesive unity within such a stable family. He has always been a vegetarian. He will have gradually and naturally assimilated the Hindu way of life during his formative years. The Hindus have no need of conversion to a religion. It is an intimate part of their way of life. From early childhood religion is fostered by rituals interspersed between the activities of each day. Each day begins with a ritual of washing; prayers are said as water is sprinkled through the fingers in worship to the rising sun, the giver of life. A little fresh water is always poured away as a sign that a man offers his labour each day without looking for any rewards. Only then will he take food, leaving a little uneaten to remind him of charity. Often a Hindu will pay a visit to a temple before beginning work. He is given a token of kindness or beneficence, usually a sweetmeat or a flower (prasad), by the temple priest. This worship may be repeated several times a day, at dawn, mid-day and sunset. In this way a child will subconsciously acquire a naturally reverent attitude towards all creation and a vision of the ultimate purpose of life. Daily worship is supplemented by the observance of sacred fasts and festivals. The women in the family are the natural guardians of traditional worship. They are keepers of the family conscience : they will keep all the main fasts, see that the household gods are venerated and will give alms to wandering holy men. Prayer is also offered for the attainment of the perfection of the soul through regeneration. Hindus do not expect to reach their goal in the space of one lifetime and they willingly accept the idea of reincarnation as they say :

'I take my duties put upon me by my past and as myself in the present and as my being, in the future through my generation.'[1]

As a child the Maharishi will have grown up in this naturally religious environment. When he grew to manhood he studied at the University of Allahabad, gaining his degree in physics. While still a student he met the man who was to be his teacher for thirteen years, 'His Divinity' Swami Brahamananda Saraswati. This man had spent most of his adult life as a solitary monk. Eventually he had been persuaded to become Shankachayara of the monastery of Jyotir Math. He was venerated for his wisdom. Dr Radhakrishnan, the philosopher and one-time president of India, addressed him as Vedanta Incarnate. Poets called him a personified divinity. The Maharishi became one of his favoured

pupils. It was from the Swami Saraswati that he learnt
the technique and meaning of TM. The Swami became
the Maharishi's personal guru. The relationship between
the master, or guru, and his pupil is an intimate one.
The guru is the absolute master of the disciple whose
reverence for his teacher is expressed in these words:

'Guru Brahma, Guru Vishnu, Guru Devo Mahesh-
varaha, Guru Sakshat, Parama-Brahma, Tasmii Shree
Guru-ve naman.'

This is translated:

'I bow down in homage to my guru (preceptor) who
not only represents the Trimurti (the three images of
the Trinity, Brahma, Vishnu and Shiva) but also the
whole Universe incarnate (Param-Brahma).'[2]

In Hinduism the guru chooses the path for his disciple.
The goal is the liberation of the pupil's soul from the im-
prisoning sense of maya: maya is human ignorance,
knowledge without wisdom, false ideas gained through
uncontrolled passions. When all this is accomplished the
soul can be merged with the great Spirit, Param-Atma,
the Brahm. The guru enables the disciple to evolve into a
deeper awareness of himself so that the self can discover
the Self (Atman) which is one with the Spirit (Brahman).

The Maharishi has retained his reverence for his own
guru. He often pays tribute to him and he always places
a picture of his master behind any platform from which
he speaks. The master died in 1953. His pupil moved

to Uttar Kashi and lived there as a hermit for two years. He then began to hand on the teaching which he had himself received. Slowly he gathered disciples of his own. He met with opposition in his country. On the last day of December 1957 the Maharishi started a world-wide movement to spread his teaching about TM and to bring its benefits to as many people as possible. He founded the Spiritual Regeneration Movement with the aim of spiritually regenerating everyone in the world. He chose Rishikesh, beside the Ganges river at the foot of the Himalayas, as the site of his Academy of Meditation. He began to travel. By 1961 he was in America. In 1962 he founded a branch of SRM in London. By 1971 he had completed thirteen world tours through fifty countries. He used any publicity that was available. In the middle of a life of great activity he found the time to write two books about his teaching. The first of these was, *The Science of Being and Art of Living*, published in 1963. His second book was, *A Commentary on the First Six Chapters of the Bhagavad Gita*, which appeared in 1966.

From 1961 onwards the Maharishi was increasingly successful in America and by October 1972 the numbers of people learning to meditate had reached 10,000 a month.[3] In 1967 he again arrived in England. He captured the headlines when it was known that the Beatles had begun to meditate. He took them off with him to Rishikesh. He left behind him a nation of people bewildered by what they had seen and uncertain how to react. The amount of publicity he received and the enthusiasm of some of his adherents made him suspect as a serious teacher. Nevertheless, he survived the hostility and since that time there has been a steady increase in the numbers of TM students in Britain. These are mainly young people. Some idea of what this means is apparent if we look at the figures for adult baptisms in the Church of England as reported in the Year Book for 1972. They averaged 660 each month for the whole of England, and must represent the numbers of people who take the religious teaching of the Anglican Church seriously enough to ask to become its members.[4] In the same year, on average, 500 new pupils each month were being taught to meditate. The movement has also gained strength in other countries, particularly in Germany and Norway.

The Maharishi has proved to be remarkably adept at introducing TM into all sorts of situations. He will not have the method tied to any system of religion. He insists that it is a simple technique which any one can learn. He claims that it is always beneficial. He has taught the same technique but has used different approaches to different sections of the community. As a scientist he quickly realised that in the West religious teachers were greeted with suspicion, and that Christianity was declining in influence, so he discarded religious language in favour of scientific terminology. In 1969 he inaugurated the first course in the Science of Creative Intelligence (SCI) at Stanford University, California, U.S.A. Since that time courses in SCI have been offered at twenty-five different universities throughout America. In 1971 he founded the first Maharishi International University and held his first International Symposium on SCI at the University of Massachusetts.

One of the strengths of the Spiritual Regeneration Movement and its offshoot, the Science of Creative

Intelligence, has been the Maharishi's willingness to submit his methods to scientific scrutiny. He has always encouraged his meditators to cooperate fully in scientific experiments about TM. By 1972 a great number of papers had been published on the physiological, psychological and social effects of TM in reputable journals such as the *Americal Journal of Physiology* and the *Lancet*.

In 1972 there was a new development. The Maharishi launched his World Plan. He intends to open 3600 centres throughout the world to instruct teachers in the art of communicating his methods to others, using the most modern teaching methods available. His World Plan has seven points :

1. To develop the full potential of the individual.
2. To realise the highest ideal of education.
3. To maximise the intelligent use of the environment.
4. To improve government achievements.
5. To solve the problems of crime, drug abuse and all behaviour that brings unhappiness to the family of man.
6. To bring fulfilment to the economic aspirations of individuals and society.
7. To achieve the spiritual goals of mankind in this generation.

Many would say that they have heard this kind of idealistic talk before and nothing has come of it. The Maharishi happens to believe with passion that it is possible to fulfil all these goals. He has made no mean beginning in the United States of America where he has now persuaded the Army to offer courses in TM to its soldiers.[5] He has persuaded the State of Illinois to adopt a resolution strongly urging that:

'All educational institutions, especially under State of Illinois jurisdiction, be strongly encouraged to study the feasibility of courses in TM and SCI on their campuses and in their faculties.'

The same document also urges that the Department of Mental Health be,

'encouraged to study the benefits of TM and in so far as the Drug Abuse section deems it to be practical and medically wise to incorporate the course of TM in the Drug Abuse programme'.[6]

In 1973 the Maharishi convened a world conference of mayors to meet in Switzerland to spread his ideas at more local levels. He has a sizable following of students in universities like Yale and Harvard. The Science of Creative Intelligence has become a world-wide movement, adaptable to a wide variety of people.

At the heart of this movement sits an astonishing man who is intent upon seizing whatever is good and natural in a man and improving upon it. The impact of his personality is undoubted. He is a tiny, abstemious man with immense energy which he conserves by keeping one day a week as a day of silence. He is said to sleep for only two hours each night. He is surrounded by flowers. He radiates joy and laughter. One of his English disciples describes his first meeting with him in this way:

'Maharishi himself is at first sight a disappointment. I do not quite know what I expected a great spiritual teacher to be like, but certainly I did not expect this tiny figure, constantly bubbling over with laughter. He was disconcerting; he made me think of a blob of mercury, bright and mobile, unpredictable, impossible to seize. The only thing I was sure of was that he was totally unlike anyone I had ever met. We soon realised, however, that all these superficial impressions were beside the point. It was contrary to all my instincts and habits of mind to admit such a thing, but I saw that Maharishi was so original a teacher that my normal standards of judgement were quite inappropriate.'[7]

This author is himself a British doctor, a member of the Royal College of Physicians and a trained observer of men. Many others have described the Maharishi in similar terms.

The appearance and personality of a man are finite. His teaching is more endurable. To find out more about this we have to turn to the written work of the Maharishi.

'When the Spirit of truth comes,
He will guide you into all truth.'

John 16 : 13.

'Those who themselves have seen the Truth
Can be thy teachers of Wisdom.'

Bhagavad Gita 4 : 34.

2 The message

Maharishi Mahesh Yogi is a Hindu. His cultural background is Indian. He belongs to a nation of five hundred million people and his religion is part of India's way of life.

Like many Christians before me I have found the doctrines of my own religion complicated. The task of understanding Hinduism from outside has been even more complex. I had little occasion to study Hinduism until my work as a doctor brought me into contact with many patients and some colleagues who came from Asian countries. My work with them made it important for me to understand their philosophy of life and I began to read widely. Since then I have spoken with many Hindus about their deepest religious concerns. It is as impossible to sum up Hinduism in a few words as it is to explain Christianity in a few sentences. Here, I have concentrated upon the major literature and the two concepts which have the greatest relevance to the Maharishi's teaching.

The Hindu religion is particularly difficult to understand because there is no one definitive book to which reference may be made: 'Hinduism is more like a tree that has grown gradually than like a building that has been erected by some great artist at some definite point in time.'[1] It has grown up among many different peoples with different customs. It probably started in the Indian sub-continent before that country was infiltrated by Aryans who came to it via Persia and Asia Minor in 2500–2000 BC. The Aryans brought with them a disposition to reflect deeply upon the nature of the universe. In time their oral traditions and poetic philosophy came to be written down in the books known as the Vedas. About 1000 BC a priestly class, known as Brahmins, grew up and from this time onwards the class system took hold. People found themselves consigned to castes according to birth. In theory there are only four castes. These are :

1. Brahmana.   Priests and teachers.
2. Kshatriya.   Kings, warriors, aristocrats.
3. Vaisya.   Traders, merchants, professionals.
4. Sudra.   Cultivators and servants.

In practice these developed into an immensely complex structure and the caste system has dominated Hindu life. Recent forces of democracy in India have tended to break down these rigid divisions of society, just as the class system has broken down in Britain.

HINDU LITERATURE

Upanishads

The priestly emphasis on code and ritual brought its own reaction against itself. There was a movement towards a deeper understanding of life. About 800 BC, and certainly before the birth of Buddha, the Upanishads came to be written. These centered on the fundamental nature of man, his place and meaning in the cosmic world. The Upanishads show Being as the Ultimate Reality which is imperishable and eternal. It is all pervading, the Omnipresent, Divine Being. They state that Brahman (the all pervading God) and the Atman (the Self) are one and the same. This is summed up in the phrase, 'Thou art That' (tat tvam asi). They also deal with concepts of good and evil. The language of the Upanishads was so metaphysical that ordinary men had difficulty in relating its doctrines to everyday life. It was natural that pure metaphysics should give way to codes of ethics and behaviour. The Smirites (Codes of Law) and the Epics of Ramayana (9th century BC) and Mahabharat (6th century BC) came to be written down. It is in this last work that the Bhagavad Gita is to be found.

Bhagavad Gita

In Hinduism of this historical period polytheism was giving way to monotheism. K. M. Sen makes this quite clear in his book :

'The Nameless and Formless is called by different names and different forms are attributed to Him, but it is not forgotten that He is One.'[2]

The Bhagavad Gita is one of the undisputed masterpieces of literature. It portrays the great spiritual struggle

of a human soul. It is set in the form of a dialogue between one of the Incarnations of Brahma, Krishna, and
man, Arjuna. It discusses the duties (dharma) of man.
It speaks of the highest ideals of man. It portrays the
ideals of renunciation, of selfless action undertaken without thought of reward, of personal self-discipline undertaken without motive, of liberation into the realms of the
spirit and imagination where all beauty and oneness
lie.

The Gita speaks of the Hindu belief that God is in all
things and that all things are in God. It is the spiritual
handbook of the ordinary Hindu. It guides his conduct.
This conduct finds expression in the words of Krishna as
he describes the kind of man who is dear to God:

'The man who has a good will for all, who is friendly
and has compassion; who has no thoughts of "I" or
"mine", whose peace is the same in pleasures and sor-
rows, and who is forgiving;
    This Yogi of union, ever full of my joy, whose soul
is in harmony and whose determination is strong;
whose mind and inner vision are set on me – this man
loves me, and he is dear to me.'[3]

No one can distil the wisdom of the Bhagavad Gita in
a few sentences. It has to be read on its own merits. It
contains precepts of exceptional beauty such as the following:

'But they for whom I am the End Supreme, who surrender all their works to me, and who with pure love
meditate on me and adore me – these I very soon

deliver from the ocean of death and life-in-death, because they have set their heart on me.

Set thy heart on me alone, and give me thy understanding: thou shalt in truth live in me hereafter.'[4]

It also contains passages which broadly are very similar to passages of practical wisdom in Christian literature:

'He who offers to me with devotion only a leaf or a flower or even a little water, this I accept from that yearning soul because with a pure heart it was offered for love.'

'Whatever you do or eat, or give, or offer in adoration, let it be an offering to me; and whatever you suffer, suffer it for me.'[5]

HINDU CONCEPTS

In the centuries after the Gita, Hinduism saw the splitting off from it of Buddhism and Jainism. These offshoots arose at a time of increasing materialism when many of the accepted tenets of Hinduism, such as the existence of God and reincarnation, were already being challenged. Buddhism influenced the Hindu way of life profoundly and for a time in the third century BC it became the state religion of India. Many of its ideas were assimilated by the older religion. It has been characteristic of Hinduism that it absorbs what is best from any religion and culture. The coming of Islam to India in the eleventh century AD led to many exchanges of ideas.

C

Modern men like Gandhi have happily absorbed some of Jesus' teaching, and made it their own. It has been this capacity to absorb ideas which has led to a remarkable lack of rigidity and an intellectual freedom among Hindus. These qualities are admired by many who are tied to the doctrines and to the traditions of the institutional structures which are found in formalised Churches.

The impersonal and personal God

The gradual development of Hinduism, and the freedom of its adherents to follow their own versions of the truth, make it impossible to say exactly what a modern Hindu believes in. A man may worship God in his own way. In the end all roads lead to the same One God. A Hindu worships an impersonal God, Brahma. He will also recognise that God is not only impersonal but personal. The personal God is represented by the trinity of Brahma, Vishnu and Siva. Brahma is the creator. Vishnu is the preserver and sustainer of the universe. Siva is the source of creative energy and also of its ultimate destruction for the sake of the further reconstruction for its own good. Within this overall trinitarian concept many incarnational expressions of the Godhead are to be found. The best known of these are Rama and Krishna who are incarnations of Vishnu. The Hindu believes that the idols and household gods are a concrete image of the Abstract. They are symbols of reality and are worshipped not as themselves but as representations of God.

Reincarnation

The other central theme of importance for a Hindu is the belief in reincarnation or the transmigration of souls. The ultimate personal goal for any man is his own absorption into God. It is thought that it would be quite impossible for this process to take place in one lifetime. The theory is that when an imperfect man dies he will be born again into a new body to continue his pilgrimage towards absorption into God. There are three main ways of reaching God. There is the path of knowledge (jnana), the path of action (karma), and the path of devotion (bhakti). Every action has its effect and every action rebounds upon its author. A good action done in one life may be rewarded in another even if the two events are thousands, or even millions of years apart. The self that a man recognises as his own is not his true Self for a man can be in a state of imperfection and then he is bound by his own passions. Man can be deceived by 'maya', a term used to indicate the tendency, through ignorance, to identify ourselves with our apparent selves in a universe which we perceive only through finite eyes. If there is an apparent self there must also be a real Self. The task of a man is to know his Self and to recognise that the Self (Atman) is at one with God (Brahman). There is, therefore, a duty (dharma) laid upon a man to seek his own perfection. Salvation depends upon oneself in successive lives. Our acts determine our characters and in turn our characters determine our acts. Each individual knows that it is his responsibility to seek his own salvation and release from the necessity of returning to the body.

It is in his own interest to seek good, to be released from ignorance and to lift his own soul to that state in which he is absorbed into God.

MAHARISHI'S TEACHING

It is against this background that Maharishi's teaching must be seen. He is a Hindu monk of the school of devotion (bhakti). He is steeped in Indian literature. He is also a twentieth-century scientist, educated as a physicist. His illustrations are often drawn from his knowledge as a scientist.

The first part of Maharishi's first book is concerned with the meaning of Being. He says:

'The science of Being, like every other science, starts its investigations into the truth of existence from the gross, obvious levels of life and enters into the subtle regions of experience. The science of Being, eventually transcends these subtle regions and arrives at the direct experience of the transcendental field of eternal Being.'[6]

He goes on to consider the nature of that abstract concept of Being. Much of his thinking about it is contained in the following passage about Being as the basis of living:

'We rarely consider, however, on what our thinking depends. Thinking is the basis of doing; what is the basis of thinking? To think we have at least to be. Being is the basis of thinking, and thinking is the basis

of doing. Being is the basis of all living. Just as without
sap there would be no root and no tree, so also without Being there would be no thinking and no doing.
There would be no living without Being. If we take
care of the sap the whole tree will flourish.

Similarily if we take care of Being the whole field
of thinking and doing will flourish. The whole field of
life can be glorified by consciously taking care of
Being.'[7]

His illustrations of the nature of Being in creation are
drawn from his knowledge of physics:

'The essential content of gas, water and ice is the same
but it changes its properties. Even though the properties of gas, water and ice are quite dissimilar, the
essential constituents, hydrogen and oxygen, are always
the same. As the oxygen and hydrogen, remaining in
their never changing states, are found exhibited in
different qualities, so also Being, remaining in Its never
changing, eternal, absolute character, is found ex-
expressing Itself in the different forms and phenomena
of diverse creation.'[8]

For the Maharishi, as for any Hindu, Being is at the
centre of the human mind. It is Atman. It is Brahman.
It can be reached by going into the inner experience of
the mind. He postulates that:

'Being cannot be experienced through any of the
senses. This shows that through whichever sense of experience we proceed we must first reach the ultimate
limit of experience through that sense. Then, trans-

cending that, we will reach a state of consciousness in which the experiencer no longer experiences.'[9]

This is to say that what is absolute cannot be perceived by the finite. In Hindu thought activity (karma) is opposed to the essential nature of Being. According to the Maharishi there is only one way to minimise the activity of experience so that one arrives at the state of Being. The process of bringing the attention to the level of transcendental Being is known as the system of Transcendental Meditation.

TRANSCENDENTAL MEDITATION

In the Maharishi's thought we can see that TM is a technique for enabling the mind to go beyond itself, beyond the apparent self to the reality and so to begin to find the state where self and reality become Self and Being. In turn Self can become one with the ultimate reality Brahman. The effects of the journey inwards are:

'The mind loses its individuality and becomes cosmic mind; it becomes omnipresent and gains pure eternal existence. In the state of the transcendent it has no capacity for experience. Here the mind does not exist, it becomes existence. When the mind returns to the field of relative life it regains individuality but retains some of the great, unbounded universal status which it had attained.'[10]

This is the principle which enables TM to be described as a method of attaining deep rest, a method of relaxation which is succeeded by an increased sense of well-being and enhanced energy.

Transcendental consciousness

The Maharishi says that in meditation a fourth state of consciousness is reached. This is called transcendental consciousness. It is a state of restful wakefulness, a state of pure awareness and is thus different from the well known states of wakefulness, dreaming sleep and dreamless sleep. It is with this fourth state of consciousness that the Science of Creative Intelligence is principally concerned. When men take up SCI they seek and get the physical benefits of TM. David Sykes, an American lawyer, sees the Science of Creative Intelligence as providing the theory to explain the practical techniques of TM. SCI explains why Transcendental Meditation should work as it does, releasing more energy, more creativity and more intelligence for everyday use.[11]

It is not necessary to have any religious background to appreciate that there might be a state beyond active thought, a state so restful that it would be logical to suppose that there are benefits if you reach such a degree of relaxation.

When a person reaches this state of consciousness he might be aware of it momentarily, just as a fish thrown back into the sea might be aware of the change from air to water, but once he has reached transcendental consciousness the meditator will cease to be aware of anything. He is. That is all.

A devout Hindu searches for the Absolute. He does not

meditate in order to gain the immediate physical benefits but in order to be united to God. In the same way the Christian tries to pass beyond the transient experience to the truth. In the Maharishi's teaching there are three more states of consciousness and each of them is important.

Cosmic consciousness

When someone has learnt to meditate he discovers that by the use of regular periods of meditation twice a day he becomes relaxed and he is able to hold on to a state of restful alertness for a time outside the immediate time of meditation. Then the effects of the pressures of life again take hold and pure awareness becomes obscured. With practice there comes a time when the state of transcendental awareness and the life of activity can co-exist. To this state of dual awareness the Maharishi gave the name of 'cosmic consciousness'. Once fully established cosmic consciousness is maintained throughout life. The Maharishi sees this state as the normal consequence of persevering in meditation. He states that it is within the reach of any ordinary man and he regards any state below cosmic consciousness as being a subnormal type of human consciousness.

The man who is established in cosmic consciousness behaves quite normally. He retains his likes and dislikes and he continues to live a life of activity. The only new awareness is that the Self is seen to be independent of activity. This Self is at rest, yet paradoxically activity continues. Cosmic consciousness is rather like being at the centre of a vortex. It is still at the centre and yet this centre is enclosed in a spinning field of activity : one state cannot exist in separation from the other.

There is a real sense in which cosmic consciousness can be described in terms of liberation. The Self is no longer bound to the relative world and is free. It might be thought that in this state the real Self could stand apart from the apparent self. By doing that the Self would be immune from the consequence of any action carried out at the direction of that part of the mind of which a man is conscious. If that were so then a man's responsibility for his own actions would be called into question. The Maharishi denies that this happens. He says that the quality of a man's actions depends upon his level of actual awareness and not upon the Self in cosmic consciousness.

Cosmic consciousness is a balanced state of mind. According to the Maharishi it cannot be reached by creating a forced mood of equanimity in all circumstances. It can only be reached through gaining the kind of timeless contentment that comes from meditation. In saying this he is opposing the views of some of the older teachers who hold that cosmic consciousness belongs only to the path of renunciation followed by the recluse who strives to become detached from all human emotions. For the Maharishi the only proper way to cosmic consciousness is through the experience of the transcendent :

'We may say that there is only one step on the path to this state of cosmic consciousness : a step out of the field of action into the transcendent and back to action again.'[12]

He does not, of course, deny that this path can be taken by recluses but he does say that the ordinary man can take this journey as well as any holy man. He emphasises that this state cannot be learnt from description of it but only through direct experience. It cannot easily be understood except by those who have some understanding of the independence of the Self from activity while the relative self continues to act. The Maharishi pictures two men climbing a mountain. If the guide keeps shouting messages about where he himself is standing it won't help the man below who is trying to climb his own bit of the mountain; it will only muddle him. The guide has to remember the route and describe the level where the man below is at so as to make him aware of his immediate surroundings and in this way help him to go higher.

When a man has become permanently established in cosmic consciousness then he is held to be free from the influence of the relative life. Such a man is free from sin and lives as an expression of the divine life.

The man who comes to cosmic consciousness is a well balanced integrated man who is no longer bound to relative experience. Such a man is unshaken by pleasure and pain, fear and anger :

'One who practises TM experiences the bliss which fills the heart and brings eternal contentment, which leaves no room for any negative emotion, for sorrow, depression fear or the like. Neither does it leave room for ways of joy or other positive emotions because the heart is by nature full and contented. It is like the heart of a grown man remaining unaffected by the toys which create great emotions in the hearts of children.'[13]

He goes on to say :

> 'This does not imply that the man of established in-
> tellect is cold and without warmth of heart. On the
> contrary, he alone is a man of full heart. He is an un-
> bounded ocean of love and happiness. His love and
> happiness flow and overflow for everyone in like man-
> ner; that is why he has no undue fondness towards
> anything.'[14]

Cosmic consciousness is one necessary step towards
what the Maharishi calls God consciousness. When
stability has been attained cosmic consciousness develops
into God consciousness through devotion (bhakti). TM
is the realisation of only one aspect of reality, that is pure
consciousness is the unmanifested absolute aspect of
reality. If a man desires to know the whole truth about
life, experience of the absolute has to go hand in hand
with the experience of relative existence. Action becomes
an important aspect of the life of devotion in the enlightened man. The Maharishi distinguishes two types of
people, the active and the contemplative. He says that
the two types of person arrive at the higher states of being
only if they are true to their own natures. The thinker
must follow the path of contemplation, the householder
the path of activity within the world. Thought and
activity are both seen as the same karma. Only good
actions, taken in harmony with a man's natural evolution towards perfection, can help him to attain to God
consciousness and ultimate release from the bondage of
life. Trying to be what you are not by nature, and cannot
be, is useless and may be harmful. He discourages the

active man from trying to become a thinker and the thinker, or recluse, from becoming active. Both will make a mess of things if they try to move into each other's territory.

The movement from cosmic consciousness to God consciousness involves surrender to the almighty will of God.

God consciousness

'Cosmic consciousness develops into God consciousness through devotion, the most highly refined type of action, which unites in the light of God the two separate aspects of cosmic consciousness, the Self and activity.'[15]

Progress in the spiritual life after the stage of cosmic consciousness repeats the sequence of events by which cosmic consciousness was established but this time not in regard to the Self but to the external world. It is a kind of looking out on the world with the mind of God. In this state the subject is not aware of God; he is God. The Maharishi moves from the discussion about the Absolute, Impersonal, Nameless One to the concept of a personal God. In some sense the world becomes suffused with the divine and takes on a quality of the Absolute. This uniting of the absolute and the world makes God no longer impersonal but personal. The nearest thought, that I can understand as a Christian, to this idea is that of Teilhard de Chardin's idea about Christification and the en-Godding of all creation. The Maharishi says that it is not a question of what you believe in: it is a question of what

you experience. He feels that God can be experienced
directly :

'God in personal form is the supreme Being of almighty nature. It is not "It" but can only be "He" or
"She". "He" or "She" has a specific form, a specific
nature, certain attributes and certain qualities. To
some the personal God is "He" and to others "She".
Some say it is both "He" and "She" but certainly it
is not "It" because of the personal character. "It",
as we have seen, belongs only to the impersonal aspect of God.'[16]

The path to God consciousness necessarily involves the
activities of a person. For Maharishi, as for every Hindu,
every action has its eternal consequence. The action rebounds upon a person just as a rubber ball rebounds
when it is thrown against a wall. Moreover there is always a close relationship between the subject and object
of any action. A good man reflects his goodness and that
quality is absorbed by those with whom he interacts. An
evil action evokes evil in the man who suffers from its
effects. In common with many other people the Maharishi
believes that an action leaves a trace even upon in-
animate objects. The memory trace of evil can be left in a
place which has seen evil men doing evil actions, and
similarly holy men and good actions can leave their im-
press on a place for thousands of years. For the Maharishi
the man who attains cosmic consciousness leaves behind
him actions which can only bring blessings to men. Such
a man is able to communicate his sense of the Absolute in
such a way that the personal God can be experienced at

a sensory level and He becomes the living Reality of daily life. Like so many men who claim to have direct personal experience of God the Maharishi finds it difficult to understand the doubts of those who have not had this experience. For him the existence of a personal God is self evident.

Union

When a man has lived in a state of God awareness for some time his perception, even of God, is changed and even understanding is transcended. As the union between God and the worshipper becomes more complete the distinction between the two becomes less easy to perceive. In the state of complete union God can no longer be the object of worship because the two are so merged that the devotee looks out on the world with the eyes of God. It is difficult for us to have a very clear idea of what this state of union with God must be like, although, as we shall see later, the mystics of every religion have sought to describe this sort of experience. The Maharishi says that this state can only be understood by those who themselves have attained to it. He believes that they are the most fortunate of men and that they rise above all limitations of race and religion so that they spread enlightenment to the whole world.

The Maharishi teaches about these seven states of consciousness on the path towards Union with God. The relationships between these states and the states described by mystics of other religious traditions will be considered later. The Maharishi postulates that his teach-

ing can be validated through a thorough knowledge of
the six systems of Indian philosophy, Myanya, Vaishes-
hika, Sankhya, Yoga, Nimansa and Vedanta. He does
not claim to teach new truth, only to rediscover the great
truths of the Bhagavad Gita and to enable ordinary men
and women to live by these principles.

There are two other strands of thought in the
Maharishi's teaching which are important for an understanding of Transcendental Meditation. One concerns
practical wisdom. The other concerns suffering.

Practical Wisdom

Apart from the main teaching about the fourth state of
consciousness and its succeeding steps towards Union
there is an important thread of common sense teaching
running through the Maharishi's work. In the second
part of his first book, *The Science of Being and Art of
Living*, the Maharishi concentrates on practical ways of
living. He covers a whole range of subjects which might
be of interest, such as the art of speaking. He uses
phrases which have a familiar ring: 'Speak according
to the moment.' 'Speak in accordance with your own
circumstances.' 'Do not speak impulsively.' When he
speaks about health he uses illustrations taken from an
observation about nature and says that it is far more
important to tend the roots of a tree than to fuss over
a withered leaf on one of the branches.

In a section about right and wrong he concentrates on
the positive qualities of human nature. For instance he
says:

'In life it is a great art to see the good in others. Everyone has some good in him.'[17]

'It is very necessary not to harm anyone. This is the least a man can do; the best that he can do is to produce an influence of harmony, goodness, kindness and helpfulness.'[18]

On reading the Maharishi's work it is noticeable that he speaks positively. He takes comparatively little notice of evil and does not stop to consider its manifestations for very long. Instead he speaks about the positive aspects of human nature, of ways in which a man can live in harmony with himself and his environment and of ways of acting which will bring him to a state of enlightenment.

Suffering

This same detachment from the negative aspects of life is also apparent when the Maharishi speaks of suffering. He holds that a man need not suffer in life. His theories on suffering are directly related to his concept of relative existence and absolute Being. He agrees that there is suffering on the relative plane. In cosmic consciousness, however, when the experience of Self coexists with relative experience, the Self is remote from the suffering. This detachment diminishes actual suffering and in the end, when the Self infuses all relative activity, suffering is no longer felt at all. He makes this claim :

'All suffering in life would be alleviated if Being were to be established on the conscious level of life where discord and disunity prevail. Since there is a way to establish Being on the level of mind (TM), body and surroundings, perfect health is possible at all levels.'[19]

The principles of reincarnation influence his ideas of the causes of suffering since he holds to the belief that suffering is the result of evil actions in a past life. There is, therefore, an element of justice in a man's suffering. Whenever a man suffers he suffers from his own actions, or from the actions of others on him, even if these actions occurred thousands of years ago. This philosophy enables a man to bear his misfortune with relative equanimity. At the same time that he accepts his own responsibility for it, he understands that if he can bear it well, and perhaps even transcend it, he will become free from its bondage. Any good action will also rebound to him in a life to come, so that release from suffering will come about as a logical consequence of his action in the present moment. In any case when a man has reached the natural state of cosmic consciousness he is largely released from the effects of the relative world although he still experiences them. Again most of his analogies are positive ones. He feels that darkness can't be overcome by darkness but only by bringing light into the blackness, and that happy people dispel suffering better than those who themselves are caught up in the actual suffering.

Perhaps the hardest part of the Maharishi's teaching about suffering is that part in which he discusses the relation between creativity and suffering :

D

'It is said that poets and artists have created their most inspired work under tension. All such statements are due to ignorance and an inability to distinguish between tensions and pressures of time or circumstance. Pressures of time and circumstance can sometimes produce much finer work but only from minds that are free and relaxed, which do not become tense through this pressure.'[20]

I shall be returning to the theme of suffering later on. The Maharishi's ideas about suffering and creativity merit much thought before the Western mind can understand what the Maharishi is saying sufficiently to enter into dialogue with him.

Throughout his oral and written teaching the Maharishi says that the gateway to the higher states of consciousness is Transcendental Meditation. This natural simple process, once started, proceeds without effort towards its own greatest happiness, its Being. It is only necessary to begin.

'Come to me all who labour and are heavy laden,
And I will give you rest.'

Matthew 11 : 28.

'When a man surrenders all desires that come to
the heart and by the grace of God finds the joy
of God, then his soul has indeed found peace.'

Bhagavad Gita 2 : 25.

3 The method

You cannot learn Transcendental Meditation out of a book. It is only taught individually by recognised teachers. The Maharishi has always insisted on this because he does not want the method to fall into disrepute through it being mis-learnt. Although he says that the technique is easy, and can be learnt by anyone who has an intact nervous system, he knows that human beings are complex enough to become muddled by the very simplicity of the method. Each person is different from any other. Each has different problems on the way to transcendental consciousness so each person needs his own guide to show him the way.

It is quite easy to find out about the initial stages of learning to meditate. In Britain the Spiritual Regeneration Movement advertises its introductory lectures. Its headquarters staff in London welcome enquirers. SRM's best advertisers are former pupils who meditate themselves and who spread their enthusiasm by word of mouth.

Anyone who wants to learn TM will find that he has to be committed. He quickly finds out that it will cost money and time and that it will involve sacrifice and obedience. This commitment is important. The fact that it will cost a week's wages to learn to meditate means that people who are merely curious, or who think it would be rather fun to learn 'just for the kicks', are discouraged. Those who anticipate that the time and money will be well spent are those who are likely to find the experience valuable. The fees are on a sliding scale, according to means. Students and old age pensioners are only asked to pay about £8.00–£10.00. Working adults are asked to donate a sum related to one week's net income. This is ordinarily not less than £25.00. SRM is a registered charity and no one in genuine financial difficulty is ever turned away. Besides the offering of money there has to be some sacrifice of time. No one can just walk in off the street and learn to meditate in an afternoon, between lunch and tea. Most people find their way to an introductory lecture at which the principles of TM are explained and the benefits are outlined. There is no fee for this lecture. Those who are interested are asked to return for a second lecture at which the mechanics of the technique are more fully explained. At this stage the potential pupil is asked to commit himself. He is expected to give up non-prescribed drugs for fifteen days before beginning to learn. He is also asked to write down his reasons for wanting to meditate. He is allocated to his teacher. He finds that he will have to give time to his studies. The first session with an individual teacher will last between one and one and a half hours. There are further follow up sessions on three consecutive days to see that the technique is established.

Before anyone starts to learn to meditate he has to go through an initiation ceremony. The aspirant brings to his teacher flowers, fruit, a white handkerchief and his fee. The teacher offers these and gifts of his own in a simple ritual ceremony before teaching begins. This ceremony is mandatory. It is intended to demonstrate that the teaching has been received from a line of teachers. The teacher stands in a tradition which stems originally from Hinduism. The sound used as a 'mantra' will be Sanskrit. It is not necessary for the pupil to be involved in the ceremony himself. It is something he observes but which he need not actually believe in. Most people, I am told, do not mind this ritual, and for some the scent of incense and the Eastern flavour of the ceremony are helpful.

The pupil is then given his 'mantra'. This is a Sanskrit sound which is specially chosen for the pupil by his teacher. It has no meaning, or if it has one the teacher will not say what it is. Because it is meaningless there are no thought associations to distract the mind. The only way to find out why a particular sound is given to a particular person is to become a teacher yourself. The 'mantra' is considered to be very important. It will be used internally and will always carry the pupil from the waking state to the fourth state of consciousness. It is interesting that sound should be used for this purpose. It is well known that during anaesthesia hearing is the last of the senses to lose consciousness. Although in TM the meditator remains awake the use of sound as a 'mantra' presumably takes the mind to the furthest limit of sensory perception.

A beginning has been made. From this point on the technique is indescribable because each person develops in such different ways. It is certain that trust and obedience have been invoked before the student has ever reached this starting point. The surrender of money and initiative into the hands of a teacher creates a relationship of mutual responsibility, and, initially, of dependence of pupil on guru. The pupil is encouraged to disclose his experiences as he goes along so that difficulties can be straightened out. He is helped to persevere.

The student closes his eyes and lets the 'mantra' pull him down into the silence. Teachers of the method agree that initially the mind tends to wander. The busier a man is, the busier are his thoughts. The meditator doesn't try to destroy them by intense concentration but after a while gently returns to the unvoiced 'mantra' as a subtle replacement. With practice the thoughts die away. They are replaced by an 'emptiness' which each man must experience for himself. The title of one long article on TM captured this well: 'You don't know you're there, but you know you've been'.[1] Words fail to indicate to outsiders precisely what has happened. Meditators are not anxious to talk about their journey inwards. They often treasure their 'mantra' as a special gift; talking about it would destroy something that is precious to them.

The best descriptions of the immediate sensations during and after meditation are simple. Words like serenity, warmth, wholeness and happiness recur in the post-meditation phase. TM is not an exotic experience. Often nothing at all appears to happen. This may be rather disappointing when one has spent time and energy learning the unaccustomed art of total relaxation; but with an individual teacher the matter is usually put right quite easily. Tired people may fall asleep. This only shows how tired they are. Tense people may have difficulty relaxing at all and this is also true of some people who have high intellects. All preconceived ideas are hindrances.

Anyone can be taught to meditate. Some people take longer than others to learn. With perseverance all can and most do learn.

The first instruction lasts about one and a half hours. The pupil is asked to meditate on his own for twenty minutes the same day and to continue afterwards by meditating for the same length of time twice a day. The next day and for two further days at least, he returns to his teacher and describes his experiences. In this way he is helped to recognise the route towards transcendental consciousness. Faults are corrected, encouragement is given and happiness is effortlessly discovered. The large majority of people are successful within the initial four day training period. If they do run into difficulties they are encouraged to go on by their friends who describe their own increased sense of well-being after meditation. It seems worth a bit of effort to gain these benefits. Some meditators have persevered for as long as eighteen months before they have really learnt the right way. The one important qualification to be able to meditate is that one has to have an intact nervous system. The Maharishi explains this:

'It is necessary to know that the whole process of TM consists in experiencing subtle states of thinking, and that because thinking depends primarily upon the physical state of the nervous system any factor which influences the physical condition of the nervous system directly influences the process of meditation.'[2]

Teachers, to whom I have spoken, say that they do not teach TM to anyone who is seriously ill with organic brain disease which affects thinking, nor to anyone with severe thought disturbance. Thought disturbance may occur in patients with florid schizophrenia or severe psychotic manic depressive illness. On the other hand these same teachers claim that people with mild reactive depression lose their depression after meditation and that people with controlled schizophrenia also benefit from the practice. The Maharishi is keen that meditators shall live a balanced life so that they do not get overtired and thus unable to experience the subtle levels of thinking which lead to the state of transcendental consciousness.

The teacher of TM is a trained person. He is trained to teach a special kind of meditation. He is not interested in the meditator's life style, moral code, profession or religion. Once the method is taught correctly and thoroughly assimilated the teacher is content to let the results speak for themselves. The Maharishi makes a definite statement that the experience of meditation effects changes in a person's life. He says:

'The system of meditation is the most effective way to bring the mind to the field of transcendental Being, where it will naturally acquire life energy for performing any amount of hard work and for producing the most effective and desirable results. This drawing of energy from the field of Being is the most striking aspect of the art of living, for it brings the active life of the day to day world into communion with the source of limitless life-energy, power, intelligence, creativity and bliss.'[3]

Again and again he and his disciples insist that TM is

easy; it is effortless; it is refreshing. He repeatedly denies
that bliss consciousness is difficult to reach, or is a state
which is reserved for the man who has renounced all
pleasure for the sake of this one pearl of great price. In
this connection he reiterates:

'It should be remembered that it does not need a long
time of silent meditation to reach Transcendental Being; just a dive within the self for a few minutes and
the mind is infused with the nature of pure consciousness which keeps it enriched through all the activities
of the day. This is the way to live the spiritual life,
which makes glorious even the physical and material
aspects of life in the world.'[4]

People who have learnt to meditate have become
enthusiastic. They have discovered a good thing for themselves and want to share it with other people. One of
their strengths lies in their ability to submit their method
to scientific tests. These tests show that the Maharishi's
technique does produce measurable physical effects, both
in the short term and over longer periods.

PHYSIOLOGICAL EFFECTS

The physiological effects of TM are being thoroughly
studied. In the Spring of 1973 forty-nine separate
scientific projects were in progress all over the world. This
work had been stimulated by earlier papers. The best
known of these was a report by two respected scientists,
Drs Wallace and Benson of the Harvard Medical Unit,

Boston, Massachusetts. They carried out their studies on thirty-six volunteers, ranging in age from seventeen to forty-one. Twenty-eight of them were men and eight were women. Each subject served as their own control. After a period at rest they were asked to meditate for twenty minutes, after which they returned to the resting state. A battery of tests were carried out with the minimum of interference to the subjects. During meditation the following physical changes were observed :

1. There is a mean decrease in the respiration rate.
2. The metabolic rate is lowered.
3. There is a reduction in oxygen consumption.
4. There is a twenty-five per cent reduction in cardiac output.
5. There is a decrease in the arterial concentration of sodium lactate.
6. There are specific electroencephalogram (EEG) changes. During meditation the alpha waves become more prominent and get deeper in the central and frontal regions of the brain. Theta waves, usually found during sleep, appear sporadically in the frontal regions.
7. There is an increase in the skin galvanic response. (This indicates a decrease in anxiety.)
8. There is a faster reaction time.[5]

This work has been confirmed by other studies, notably Allison's in England.[6] He worked on respiratory rates in TM subjects. Dr P. Fenwick, of the Maudsley Institute in London, worked on the EEG changes in meditators.[7] These results have been given in full because they show the extent of the research carried out. To obtain such results the subjects had electrodes fastened to them. Needles were inserted in their arms to tap the arterial blood flow and polygraphs were made during the period of experimentation. The results were calibrated and precisely recorded.

The most significant change in body function is the decrease in the metabolic rate. This means that the body consumes less energy and all the life processes are slowed down. The subject is in a state of deep relaxation.

The decrease in blood lactate is also significant. Patients with anxiety neuroses respond to external stress with an excessive rise in blood lactate level. Likewise if sodium lactate is injected into the blood stream the patient becomes very anxious. TM, however, produces quite opposite effects: these indicate relaxation.

On average, people who meditate regularly have lower blood pressures than those who do not. It is known that patients with high blood pressures have high blood lactate levels. It must be noted that blood pressure levels changed very little during meditation, but then none of these subjects was hypertensive at the time of the experiment.

The EEG changes are unique. Patterns which normally are found only in alert people coexist with changes normally found in sleep. Some of these results have been found as well in people who use Zen meditation and relaxation techniques of yoga. Y. Sugi and K. Akutsu studied Zen meditators in New Delhi.[8] Anand, G. S. Chinna and Balden Singh examined yogi, meditating in a closed box, using a relaxation technique of meditation.[9] In all these subjects the metabolic rate was lowered.

Predominance of alpha waves, especially in the frontal and central regions of the brain, were noted on the E.E.G. It was only in the very experienced Zen masters, mainly those who had meditated for over twenty years, that theta waves (6–7 cycles per sec.) appeared. In TM subjects these theta waves were found in people who had meditated for as little as six months.

The pattern of physiological changes during the actual meditation suggests that meditation starts as an integrated response in the central nervous system. This response is the opposite of the fight-flight response by which the body responds to stresses by the arousal of the sympathetic reflexes. The neuro-psysiological state of people during meditation is one of alert relaxation.

PSÝCHOLOGICAL EFFECTS

The physiological changes during meditation are precise. It is less easy to specify the psychological effects because of the number of variable factors in any single experiment. Most of the psychological work has been done on performance times, learning ability and perceptual ability. There are currently sixty different research projects into the psychological effects of TM. These range from studies on the value of using TM as an adjunct to psychotherapy to complex studies of the effect of TM on self actualisation. Among the most definite results are:

1. Increased perceptual ability. (Tested on the hearing sense.)

2. Superior perceptual motor performance. (Speed and accuracy of performance.)
3. Increased learning ability.
4. Personality inventory tests tend to show that subjects who meditate display reduced nervousness, aggression, depression, irritability, tension, tendency to dominate and self-doubt. These people tend to show an increased sociability, self-awareness, outgoingness, staying power and efficiency.

All these scientific results are summed up in the enthusiastic response of some individual meditators. One man reported that he looked and felt better. He had fewer quarrels with his wife. His mind felt clear. His patience increased.[10] An American reported that he became much more aware of colours: 'Red seemed redder, there are more shades of red. It is as if I had been looking at the world in smudged glasses that are now clean.' This man is a devout Catholic. He feels a new man as a result of his meditations and knows himself to be a changed one:

'It's as if my mind has a lever and is four times as potent, relaxed, rested. I read more, enjoy more. My mind has become a sponge. I see people pushing in train stations, or parents berating their children, and realise I used to be like that. Now I take more time, and almost feel sorry for people who had a terrible need to hurry everywhere. My religion also means more to me now. And the change in me changes the people I touch. I am suddenly becoming the man I always wanted to be but never knew how.'[11]

In personal communications to me many people have spoken of an increased sense of peace, a harmony which has somehow been lacking in their lives before.

These accounts breathe life into the bare bones of the scientific results. They also highlight one of the facts about TM. It is not an activity done in isolation from the rest of the meditator's life. It profoundly affects their way of life. The Maharishi stresses the necessity of a balanced life for the man who meditates. TM enables people to change their way of life. As the result of sitting down for twenty minutes twice a day they have to stop rushing about. They find the experience pleasurable and many later question the rightness of a life of perpetual activity and strain. Consequently they want to develop. The things which were once so important to them, like material success, money and pleasure, become relatively unimportant compared with the deep sense of inner peace which they find through TM. The disciple tries to live in a balanced and harmonious way and he takes steps to achieve this by bringing his new insights to bear on the whole of his life. The Maharishi has many practical suggestions for people who want to cultivate this peace in their lives. He says that it is important to take life naturally and easily, for a peaceful mind helps the meditator to arrive at the transcendental state more quickly. He advises people to choose the right kinds of food and the right type of activity which does not over-excite the nervous system. The Maharishi never places any emphasis on 'Thou shalt not' injunctions. He finds that the mind naturally seeks its state of greatest happiness. The meditator will want to return to that sort of happiness. This is the reason why he will return to

meditation at regular intervals. This is why he changes
his way of life so as to preserve that happiness. This is
why a man will even give up drugs.

SOCIAL EFFECTS OF TM

One of the most important claims of the Science of
Creative Intelligence is that TM helps people to give up
the use of drugs. In the United States of America there
are twenty research projects going on to try to define the
use of TM in drug abuse programmes. In a paper presented to an international medical conference at
the University of Michigan, Drs Wallace and Benson
described their questionnaire survey of 1862 people who
had used drugs before they took up TM. Of these people,
eighty per cent had used marijuana, forty-eight per cent
had used LSD and smaller percentages had been on
amphetamines and heroin. After twenty-one months of
meditation more than ninety-five per cent had stopped
using drugs. Only twelve per cent of marijuana users were
still on the drug, three to four per cent were still on
LSD and less than one per cent were using other drugs.[12]
There were no controls in this series, so that scientifically
the results remain inconclusive because they were unable
to be compared with the results of other forms of therapy,
or of no therapy. In another study Winquist studied 143
people who used illegal drugs. Of the 111 people who
used hallucinogenic drugs, and the 42 people who
used 'hard' drugs, eighty-six per cent were said to have
stopped altogether and fourteen per cent to have reduced their intake of drugs after three months of

E

meditation. According to this author, forty-nine per cent of the drug users said that they managed to reduce their drug intake because life was so much more satisfying.[13] This study used a questionnaire which was filled out by the patients. There was no objective evidence as to whether they had really stopped taking drugs as they said they had. Research in this field continues. Several pilot studies have shown encouraging results, notably at the Stanford Research Institute where Dr Leon Otis found that thirty-five out of forty-nine opiate addicts were able to give up the drug after six months of TM.[14] Nearly all the reported projects at present suffer from being too small and inadequately controlled. However, research is progressing.

SPIRITUAL EFFECTS OF TM

The Maharishi is quite definite that TM is not a religion. He, himself, is a religious man. He does not question the existence of God. He says that a meditator will naturally progress from being one who meditates twice a day for the benefits it gives him to being one who attains cosmic consciousness. Then a new awareness of creation and its meaning will enable a man to say that he is in a state of God consciousness. The journey of evolution is not so much a progression upwards to what is as yet unattained, but rather is a gradual realisation of what has always been. The spiritual effects of TM are really inseparable from the effects of the mind and the body, for Being is held to influence all relative existence. Hence the physical benefits which are observable must

derive from the spiritual state of the Self (Atman)
which is at one with the Being (Brahman). Being spills
over into a whole field of life.

The Maharishi condemns those religions which base
their teaching mainly on the fear of God and he upholds
the religion of love. He states that :

'The love of God is the greatest virtue that a man can
ever cultivate; through this develops love for the
creation of God, for the children of God. Kindness,
compassion, tolerance and helpfulness to others
emanate from the heart in which the love of God
grows.'[15]

'Let not your hearts be troubled,
  Neither let them be afraid.'

                              John 13 : 27.

'For all things born in truth must die,
  And out of death in truth comes life.
  Face to face with what must be,
  Cease thou from sorrow.'

                    Bhagavad Gita 2 : 27.

4 The healing potential of Transcendental Meditation

Every medical student knows that it is easier to observe the symptoms and signs of disease than to understand their cause. It has sometimes happened that the greatest therapeutic discoveries have been made almost by chance. Doctors still use some treatments simply because they work: they do not know why the cure is effective. No scientist is content until he can fully understand how a disease arises and why a particular treatment works. It is known that Transcendental Meditation is an antidote to stress. If we are to harness its potential for the good of mankind we have to find out how it works. In this way we would have some hope of predicting how it could best help men and women. Our knowledge about both stress diseases and TM is still incomplete, but in this chapter I shall try to begin to understand how TM affects the body through the nervous system. I shall then seek to understand how stress causes disease and look at the areas where TM might be expected to be useful therapeutically.

In order to understand how TM works we have to have some knowledge of how the nervous system works.

THE NERVOUS SYSTEM

The nervous system is made up of a central nervous system, which comprises the brain and the spinal cord, and a peripheral nervous system, which is a system of nerves connecting the central parts to the tissues and organs of the body. That part of the nervous system which is outside our conscious control is called the autonomic nervous system. It controls the activity of the glands, heart, blood vessels and digestive organs. It is responsible for the effects of our thoughts and emotions on those organs which are outside conscious control. For instance, when someone is embarrassed they may blush. The sudden flood of blood to the cheeks occurs as the direct consequence of an emotion. It cannot be stopped at will because the autonomic nervous system works automatically once the incident happens. The only thing which could avert the blushing would be not to be embarrassed.

This autonomic nervous system has its most important headquarters in the brain. This is the hypothalamus. It lies under the two great lobes of the forebrain, the cerebral hemispheres, and is closely connected to the pituitary gland. The hypothalamus controls blood pressure, temperature and many other aspects of the digestive and excretory processes. It does all this via the peripheral parts of the autonomic nervous system known as the parasympathetic and sympathetic systems. Through its link with the pituitary gland the hypothalamus is involved in the functions of growth, sex, secretion of urine, and in the output of the thyroid and adrenal glands. It maintains a stable internal environment.

Physical responses to stress

The autonomic nervous system co-ordinates the physical response to a stressful situation. This is known as the fight-flight response. In any emergency situation, where a person is confronted with a threat, he has the choice between staying to grapple with the problem or running away. Either way the physical changes which take place are due to the spontaneous workings of the autonomic nervous system, principally through the outpouring of adrenalin by the sympathetic nervous system. A man who is attacked by another man will find that his body will very quickly respond to the threat. Adrenalin is poured into the blood stream. The pulse quickens. The blood pressure rises. The muscles tense to take action. The pupils dilate. A reflex surge of blood flows to the limbs and the oxygen intake is dramatically stepped up by deeper faster breathing. In a moment the two men are fighting each other, or one is taking to his heels and running away. The same physiological mechanisms are called into play whichever way he makes his choice.

Emotional responses to stress

It is known that the hypothalamus is concerned with the expression of emotion. Patients who have diseases which affect the nervous pathways between the hypothalamus and the cerebral cortex (brain surface) may show changes in their personality, usually for the worse, and display irrational outbursts of temper. The hypothalamus is connected to the cerebral cortex by a complex of nervous pathways known as the limbic system and this system is responsible for the conscious experience of emotion as distinct from its outward expression. It might be easier to understand this very complex interaction of different parts of the nervous sysem if we consider what happens to the driver of a car, when he has to take avoiding action quickly in an emergency. He sees that he is in danger. The impulses telling him this pass from all his external senses to many parts of the nervous system. Immediate reflex actions take place in the spinal cord and operate through the voluntary muscles, so that instantaneous avoiding action can be taken. Other impulses speed to the autonomic nervous system relay stations outside the central nervous system. Adrenalin pours into the blood stream. The pulse quickens and the whole sympathetic sequence comes into play. Simultaneously the hypothalamic connections alert the brain surface. The brain sends messages to the driver's arms and legs so that he can take conscious action. The outward expression on the face of the driver, such as clenched teeth, and the grimace of fear or anger, are affected through the autonomic nervous system. The awareness of these emotions takes place through the direct connections between the sensory cerebral cortex and the limbic system which connects it to the hypothalamus, the seat of the emotions. The actual awareness of fear or anger, and the consciousness that one's heart is pounding, one's mouth is dry and one's teeth are clenched, comes after the emergency is over. There is a perceptible time lag, so that it is a common experience to find that one only feels frightened and trembly after one has coped efficiently with the emergency. It is then that one driver shouts angrily at the other, or cries with relief.

The hypothalamus and sleep

In recent years neurologists have become aware of a dense concentration of cells and short nerve fibres around the upper part of the spinal cord and the hypothalamic region of the brain. These form a widespread network. The network is known as the reticular system and it is thought to be responsible for 'arousing' the cerebral cortex. It is known that if the reticular system in the brain stem is electrically stimulated, the brain waves, as recorded by the EEG, show an 'alert' pattern. There is a close correlation between states of consciousness and the intactness of the reticular system; its close connection with the hypothalamus (jointly known as the reticulo-hypothalmic system) is essential to consciousness. The reticular pathways appear to be very fast relays which alert the brain and facilitate the reception of sensory stimuli. Sometimes they inhibit responses to stimuli so that over-reaction to any particular stimulus does not take place. The reticulo-hypothalmic system is concerned in the mechanisms of sleep. The hypothalamus is involved in inducing sleep, but it does not act like a push-button mechanism so that one falls asleep automatically when the hypothalamus 'decides' the time is right. The cerebral cortex also plays some part in its own regulation. This must be one of the reasons why it is possible to win the struggle to stay awake at a lecture after lunch. If we look at the sleepy student we may be able to understand how this complex co-ordinating system works.

Impulses reach the hypolthalamus from the full stomach. These are registered and electrochemical responses ensure that more blood is diverted to the stomach to cope with the digestive processes. At the same time the student is hearing the lecturer and seeing the blackboard. These sensations travel up to the cerebral cortex. Some go direct; others go via the hypothalamus and the limbic systems (the pathways for emotions). There is an exchange of impulses in both directions, between the grey matter of the brain and the hypothalamus and its peripheral out-stations. All these stimuli are co-ordinated in the hypothalamus. If the lecture is boring or the voice monotonous, the sensory cortex is understimulated and sleep overcomes the listener. If the lecture is interesting or provocative, the student yawns (thus increasing his oxygen intake), shifts his position (thus altering his circulatory balance), and succeeds in exerting conscious control over consciousness. Any really strong emotion, like anger, will act as an intense stimulus and cause the student to sit up at once and take notice.

Consciousness

Consciousness is an integrated experience. It is built up from simpler unconscious impulses, some reaching the brain cortex by direct sensory impulses, others reaching it via the reticulo-hypothalamic pathways. It is known that consciousness is a function of the forebrain (cerebral hemispheres and diencephalon) and that below this level neural activity is unconscious.

The current thinking about consciousness springs from the knowledge that the reticulo-hypothalamic system is essential to consciousness. If the pathways are destroyed, so that there are no routes to the cerebral cortex, there are no conscious processes. On the other hand, living beings who are born without a cerebral cortex can survive, live and sleep and show signs of pleasure. The reticulo-hypothalamic system provides an integrative system which organises states of consciousness. Drugs, like hypnotics and anaesthetics, produce unconsciousness by inhibiting the activity of the ascending reticular system. Stimulants have the opposite effect.

Scientific knowledge about consciousness is far from complete. It is consistent with neuro-physiological principles to think that in Transcendental Meditation the brain functions are modified so that the activity of the connections between the hypothalamus and the cerebral cortex is reduced while, at the same time, the activity of the reticular 'arousal' system (ascending reticular system) remains alert or even becomes more active.

The fact that we may be able to tell how it is that a person remains conscious, and what the possible changes are in a person who is meditating, tells us why the technique is easy to learn. Once the route has been learnt the brain 'remembers'. Regaining the fourth state of consciousness becomes habitual, using internal 'feed back' to track along familiar neural pathways. Once the 'trigger' (mantra) has been pulled the neural pathways come into operation and the person slips easily into the state of transcendental consciousness.

Transcendental Meditation produces definite though small changes in the nervous system. These are reflected in the characteristic changes in the nervous system, as shown by the changes in the EEG patterns. The mood changes and sensations, which follow TM, are the result of the hypothalamic changes, and are the consequences of these alterations in internal balance; so are the physical effects mediated through the autonomic nervous system. This is why it is possible to predict situations in which TM will be helpful therapeutically.

Chemical changes in the brain

The nervous system is not just another electrical circuit. At numerous nerve interchanges, or synapses, complex electro-chemical interchanges take place. Chemical transmitters are released; these boost the electrical charge along the nerve. The best known of these are adrenalin, norepinephrine, and acetylcholine. These are always found in the peripheral nervous system but are also present in specific parts of the central nervous system. A less familiar chemical nerve transmitter is serotonin, which is chemically related to adrenalin. It occurs widely in the body, but in the CNS (cerebrum) it is found only in the surface grey matter of the cortex. Elsewhere the highest concentrations are in the hypothalamus, the thalamus and the brain stem where the reticular system is concentrated. The precise action of serotonin is as yet unknown. Its importance is that we now know that brain activity can be directly affected by the secretions of nerve cells, varying in kind and amount in different parts of the nervous system. For instance, gross alterations in the serotonin content of the brain can be responsible for abnormal psychic states. On this hypo-thesis schizophrenia is caused by abnormality in brain cell metabolism. So far a link between schizophrenia and abnormal serotonin metabolism has not been established. New facts are coming to light about the neuro-physiology of the brain and much research is being carried out in this biochemical field.

THE NATURE OF STRESS

Stress is one of those deceptive words which are so commonly used that we all think we know its meaning; it remains difficult to define with precision. As used technically in physics, stress is a constraining or impelling force which, applied to a physical body, causes strain. Thus a person who is subject to stress could become strained. In everyday language the two words are used interchangeably; cause and effect are lumped together but here the distinction will be preserved.

When men are faced with stress they can often draw on hidden reserves of strength to cope with the demand. They are said to adapt. For instance, a man who is in good physical shape can run a race; his body is strained to the limit of its ability but it can adapt to the demands of the stress of the race. If the man is 'out of condition' his body cannot adapt quickly; it becomes overstrained and fails under its task.

The adaptation to stress is full of hazards. Let us think what happens to a piece of elastic which is put under stress by being pulled at its two ends. The stress is applied and the elastic stretches. If you hold the two ends wide apart and apply a gradual pull, the nature of the elastic enables it to expand to the point where there is no more elasticity available. The elastic becomes overstrained and eventually breaks. If, however, the elastic is so old that it has lost its internal springiness, it breaks earlier than it would have done otherwise. Similarly, if you hold the two ends of the elastic close together and pull it with a sudden sharp jerk you can break it more easily. So you see that in any situation, what happens depends upon the interactions of a number of variable factors, including the force of the external stress, the way it is applied and the capacity of the elastic to adapt to the stress. The analogy can be applied to a man who is under stress, although the variables are multiple and more complex. In addition a man is affected by stress of his own internal making as well as by stress from outside himself. This cannot be seen in action but is none the less a deciding factor in the man's capacity to adapt to stress.

Stress always involves change. In recent years a great deal of work has been done on the failure of human beings to adapt to stress. The capacity of some individuals to absorb stress seems limitless. Men can climb to great heights, endure extremes of cold or travel in space. Their bodies are trained to adapt to the environmental demands. Nevertheless, there is a point beyond which the human body will not go. Left to itself it cannot adapt. Without oxygen a man will die at heights where the oxygen content of the atmosphere is too low to sustain life. Without protective clothing a party of schoolboys die of exposure, killed by the cold. Without a space suit an astronaut would die on a space walk. Man's scientific ingenuity has stretched the capacity of the human body and has expanded his horizons. All the same, man in his romantic attitude to adventure seems to have overlooked the fact that most human beings do not have limitless capacity for absorbing stress. Everyone has a breaking point. In the last decade there have been some fascinating discoveries about the human capacity to withstand stress. Let us look at some of the research which throws light on this subject.

At one time it was thought that all physical diseases were caused by physical agents. If you were attacked by pneumonia germs you got pneumonia with well marked organic changes in the lungs. You had a properly respectable illness. If, however, you were just a born worrier you could think you had cancer but you would not have any disease changes in the organs to show for it, and you would find that your illness was dismissed as 'functional'. You would be told cheerfully that there was nothing wrong with you, and you would be left to suffer from the symptoms of which you had complained. Over a long period of time doctors have come to wiser attitudes about illness. The idea that unhappiness and anxiety can actually produce physical illness is no longer eccentric. Illnesses in which the mind and body are closely interlinked are called psychosomatic diseases. We know that in certain conditions like asthma, high blood pressure, stomach ulcers, coronary artery disease, the emotional state of a patient is closely linked to his physical wellbeing. Psychosomatic medicine has enabled us to stop labelling illnesses as organic or functional, physical or psychological, and to start thinking in terms of disease of the whole person.

Once people had begun to realise that many diseases

F

could be caused by non-physical agents they became interested in stress as a cause of physical disease. Some researchers concentrated upon environmental stresses which could cause illness, while others looked at the internal stresses which cause a man to become ill. Here I have selected two research projects to illustrate the importance of stress as a prime cause of disease.

The idea that environmental stress could be a prime factor in illness was only given its full weight from 1960 onwards. Much of this work has been carried out in America where the pace of life is such that the young middle-aged male population has been decimated by stress diseases. At Cornell Medical Center in New York, Dr Harold Wolff had spent a lifetime teaching that the environment of a man was important to his well-being. One of his colleagues, Dr T. H. Holmes, came up with a theory that what decided whether you were ill or well was the amount of change in your life over a given period. It didn't matter whether you were subject to good changes or to bad; what mattered was the magnitude of the stress and the speed with which you had to adapt. Dr Holmes set out to put his theories to the test. With another doctor, a psychiatrist, Dr R. Rahe, he devised a system for measuring how much change an individual had experienced in a given span of time. By sampling the population they discovered what changes in people's lives were considered to be the most important. They found, for instance, that bereavement through the death of a spouse ranked as the most important change in the life of the remaining partner. This was ranked on a Life-change Unit Scale as 100, and other significant changes, like changing jobs or houses, were ranked relative to this measurement. On this scale moving house would rate twenty points. Using this Life-change Unit Scale, they questioned thousands of people and correlated their findings with the individuals' states of health. They found convincing evidence to show that people with high life-change scores were more likely to be ill, in the year following the score, than those people who had low life-change scores. The results were published in 1967.[1] Since then the experimental surveys have been repeated and in each case it has been found that there is a direct correlation between the life-change score and the subsequent development of illness. The higher ratings of life-change carry a higher risk that the subsequent illness will be severe.

In the same year that this paper appeared one of the researchers, Dr R. Rahe, began to work with a United States Navy doctor, Commander R. J. Arthur, on a prospective study of illness. They forecast sickness patterns in a group of three thousand sailors on three different cruisers. The men were about to go on a six month tour of sea-going duty. During the journeys exact records were kept of the men's illnesses. A questionnaire, given to the men before sailing, asked the sort of questions which tried to find out whether changes, either good or bad, had occurred in the men's lives during the preceding year. At the end of the six months another team of assessors, different from the one which had administered the questionnaire, looked at the medical records of all the men in the research project. By the end of their survey of sickness incidence, the facts were proven. Men in the upper ten per cent of life-change units, that is those who had to adapt to the most change in the preceding year, suffered one and a half to two times as much ill-ness as those in the bottom ten per cent.[2] Alvin Toffler quotes these experiments in his study of mass bewilder-ment in the face of accelerating change. His book, *Future Shock*, is an important work for the under-standing of the effects of stress and rapid change on individuals and on society. He quotes Dr Arthur as say-ing:

'For the first time we have an index of change. If you've had many changes in your life within a short time, this places a great challenge on your body . . . an enormous number of changes within a short period might overwhelm its coping mechanisms. It is clear that there is a connection between the body's defences and the demands for change that society imposes. We are in a continuous dynamic equilibrium . . . various "noxious" elements, both internal and external, are al-ways present, certain viruses live in the body and cause disease only when the defences of the body wear down. There may well be generalised body defence systems that prove inadequate to cope with the flood of de-mands for change that come pulsing through the ner-vous and endocrine systems.'[3]

Another facet of the same problem of stress, and the diseases it precipitates, was considered in an important survey carried out on the health of Church of Scotland clergy by Dr Hugh Eadie. He studied a representative sample of one hundred ordained parochial clergy selected from a total population of 1827. Eighty-five of these men were interviewed in 1969. The relationship between health and stress was the subject of the survey. 44.7 per cent of the men had required no medical attention during their lifetimes, except for minor illnesses. Of the others, 16.4 per cent had been receiving treatment for chronic complaints. The most outstanding feature of the interviews with these men was the high incidence among them of stress diseases and the prevalence of mental, psychoneurotic and personality disorders. Two out of three men had suffered from psychological complaints. Nervous breakdowns were commoner in men under forty-five years of age, while personality difficulties were more apparent in men over this age. The most important finding was the clear evidence which emerged from the interviews. This showed that stress arose principally out of intrapersonal conflicts and tensions. Here I quote:

'There is no doubt that the parish minister, in the experience of these men, is subject to considerable external pressures . . . these men readily identified frustrations associated with persistent, sometimes unreasonable, parishioner demands; with widespread apathy, nominalism and sheer inertia among parishioners, and the lack of support and leadership from significant lay people . . . These were the principal frustrations identified by these men. In general, they had felt enormous pressure from vocational demands, social expectations, and interpersonal conflicts. Superficially the minister appears to be the victim of insurmountable obstacles and frustrations which come from outside himself. However, while these external pressures are real enough what matters is the way in which the clergyman perceives and responds to such conditions. The real issue is the way in which he relates those external factors to himself and to his self-image.'⁴

A SUGGESTED THERAPEUTIC USE FOR TM IN STRESS DISEASES

We now have enough evidence to show that stress is one of the villains in the drama of disease. Stress may come from the environment or it may arise from within the organism. Stress which is continued for long periods of time at a low level can be sustained better than rapidly changing pressures over a short period. Stress can cause physiological changes in the body. Some of these changes can become permanent. On occasion the body goes on reacting as if stress were present even when the immediate crisis is over. The adaptive reaction fails; recovery through rest stops. The consequences may be permanent and disastrous.

One of the best ways of combating stress is, of course, to remove the stress altogether. Another, is to reduce its impact by cushioning its effects in various ways. A third way is to encourage the body to relax between stressful periods in such a way that the bad effects of stress are minimised. Days off work at fairly frequent intervals have been found to be more beneficial than one occasional prolonged holiday. Relaxation techniques have been widely used to combat stress and are effective in people who are able to learn the art of releasing all muscular and mental tension.

TM in the prevention of stress diseases

Armed with some knowledge of stress, and some aware-ness of how Transcendental Meditation works through changes in the nervous system, we can now look at the kinds of situation in which it might be expected to work to the benefit of human beings. Obviously one of the fields it might be useful in, is that of preventative medicine through the alleviation of stress by deep relaxation.

I should like to cite an instance where I think that TM could be valuable. A recent study was carried out on air traffic controllers in Chicago. These men are subject to variable stress during their tours of duty at O'Hare air-port. The pressures were closely observed and compared with the rates of excretion of substances called catechola-mines. These excretion rates reflected the body's physical response to stress. It was found that during the late part of the early morning shift (0300–0700 hrs) very high rates of excretion of catecholamines were observed. This pattern persisted during the afternoon when the controllers were off duty and asleep. In the early even-ing, when their work was again very stressful in terms of aircraft movements, adrenalin was excreted in dispro-portionately large amounts. Once the period of duty was over the excretion rate of catecholamines fell.[5] In an-other study, on records held by the Federal Air Surgeon in Washington DC, the incidence of different diseases among air traffic controllers was studied. The researchers concentrated on the incidence of high blood pressure, peptic ulcers and diabetes, all of which are known to be associated with stress. The study suggested that air traffic controllers were at special risk of developing hypertension. This risk was related to the density of air traffic movements when, it will be remembered, the earlier study had shown that the rate of adrenalin excretion was disproportionately high. There was also an increased risk of falling sick with a peptic ulcer at a younger age than usual. The data were uncertain about diabetes.[6] Now if the air traffic controllers were to meditate before their afternoon sleep, and when they went off duty, it might well be found that their overall response to stress had been modified, particularly with regard to adrenalin excretion. By returning periodically to deep rest between spells of intense activity the air traffic controllers should, theoretically, be able to withstand the stresses they meet, better over the long-term period.

The great difficulty in advocating that all air traffic controllers should learn TM lies in the known facts about the personalities of air traffic controllers. In a study of the attitudes and motivation of these men it was found that they were attracted to their jobs by its challenge, the fast pace of the operations and the constant changes they had to meet every day.[7] They might find that they were not prepared to become the kind of individuals who found meditation congenial. Everybody can meditate but not everybody wants to.

Theoretically, anxiety should respond to TM. The findings about blood lactate levels dropping during meditation indicate this. Certainly, TM meditators are shown to be less anxious than their non-meditating counterparts. Anxiety and depression are part of normal human experience. The fact that they are both mediated in the nervous system at the neuro-chemical level would lead us to believe that mild cases of anxiety and depression should respond to TM. This is, in fact, the case. Most of the published work about TM has so far related to students whose personalities were assessed as 'anxious' or 'depressed'. They were psychologically predisposed towards emotional disease but were not incapacitated to the point of illness.

There is an excellent case for thinking that TM could prevent tension and minimise the effects of stress. If it is true that meditation changes people's ways of life then they will also benefit from the healthier ways they have chosen. It is less easy to see how the technique can help people in whom disease is already well established.

Transcendental Meditation and stress disease

Disease is often a question of degree. One day the balance within the body shifts in such a way that the person changes from someone whose blood pressure is 'a little on the high side' to someone whose blood pressure is permanently raised and whose organs begin to become permanently damaged. During the early research it was hoped that TM would directly lower the blood pressure in the same way that drugs did. The drugs had unpleasant side effects while TM had none. Dr Benson, a cardiologist, had hoped that regular meditation would have been of immediate value to his hypertensive patients. However, the early experiments showed that there were only minimal falls in blood pressure during meditation itself. Dr Benson subsequently went on with long-term studies and he has produced some evidence to show that the altered behaviour which results from the practice of meditation does have an overall effect on the blood pressure levels.[8] This is presumably because of increased happiness and less strenuous efforts by the patients to achieve success. It is obvious that any technique which produces sensible living habits would have a similar effect.

In psychological medicine TM has an overall beneficial use providing that the patient has intact neural pathways and can cooperate in learning. It helps people who are anxious and depressed. Difficulties arise when, for instance, agitation is marked and sustained, so that the pathological restlessness reaches such a degree that relaxation of any sort becomes impossible. Such a patient could not meditate. However, he could benefit once the initial symptoms had been brought under control with drugs, and it has been found that patients who meditate need less medication. Again, one is reminded that prevention is better than cure and is easier if the patient perceives his danger at an early stage of his illness.

There have been few well documented studies on schizophrenia. In people with severe thought disorder we should not expect to be able to use TM, but there have been many individual reports of improvements in schizophrenics who are able to learn to meditate. As this condition often gets better of its own accord it is always difficult to assess the value of any therapy. This is one of the reasons why precise assessment of drug therapy has been so difficult in this condition.

The most interesting therapeutic use of TM, so far, has been in the field of drug abuse. Some drugs, like LSD, have a powerful effect on the sub-cortical reticulo-hypothalamic systems. The fact that TM also has effects on this area of the brain lends hope to the theory that TM might selectively cancel out the need of cells to 'want'

LSD for their well-being. There is also a chemical affinity between the hallucinogens, like marijuana and LSD, and adrenalin and serotonin. It is also known that many of the major tranquillisers, like largactil, act at this level of the brain. Relatively little research has been done in this field, and so far no long-term results are available about the effects of meditation on users of 'hard' narcotics. Young people have told me personally and enthusiastically that they have been able to stop using drugs after TM. All to whom I have spoken say that drugs become uninteresting when you have discovered a new way of life. TM is not just a therapy. It becomes a way of life.

Evaluation of TM as a therapeutic agent

Any individual may well benefit from regular periods of withdrawal from their active pursuits to meditate. I have been unable to discover any scientific data about religious meditation apart from the data I have quoted on Yoga and Zen techniques. This is a major difficulty in assessing the relative values of TM against other systems which concentrate upon periods of relaxation and rest interspersed with activity. In our present state of knowledge we simply do not know how TM compares with contemplative Christian prayer (with which it seems to have an affinity, as will be discussed in the next chapter), either in its short-term effects or in its long-term results. We have no data, either, about the catecholamine excretions of communists guarding the Brandenburg Gate nor about their Catholic counterparts on the other side of the Berlin wall.

On the other hand, we do have valuable information on the personalities of TM enthusiasts. We do have precise data on the physiology of TM. We can predict with confidence that TM has potential in the prevention of stress disease and a role as an adjuvant therapy in established disease, especially where the reticulo-hypo-thalamic system is affected by changes which are potentially reversible. The implications for society are far reaching.

The Maharishi is not the only prophet on the scene today who is telling us that the quality of life is important, that there is a limit to the amount of stress which the human body can absorb and that stress is a major threat to human happiness. People like Theodore Rosak and Alvin Toffler have much to say of our condition in society. All over the world ordinary people are questioning the assumptions upon which the scientific technological society is based. TM works at an individual level and aims to create an enlightened society through the enlightenment of its individual members. In a radical book, Dr E. F. Schumacher, one time economic adviser to the National Coal Board, faces these questions from the standpoint of an economist who takes human beings into account. He ends his book with these words:

'Everywhere people ask: "What can I actually do?" The answer is as simple as it is disconcerting: we can, each of us, work to put our own inner house in order. The guidance we need for this work cannot be found in science or technology, the value of which utterly depends on the ends they serve; but it can still be found in the traditional values of mankind.'[9]

'For he that is not against us
Is for us.'

Mark 9 : 40.

'In any way that men love me,
 In that same way they find
 my love :
 For many are the paths of men,
 But they all in the end come to me.'

Bhagavad Gita 4 : 11.

5 Affinities between Christianity and Transcendental Meditation

When I first heard about Transcendental Meditation my immediate reaction was to say to myself, 'But I already know what this is all about.' My second thought was that I had read about states of prayer which had close parallels with the descriptions of TM given to me by my friends. This chapter is concerned with the examination of those two thoughts to see how much truth there was in them.

Personal experience

Life in the twentieth century is so crowded with people and events and it goes so fast, that sometimes it is hard to preserve any real sense of value as an ordinary person. We feel rather like specks of sand on the seashore. In itself the speck is tiny, almost too insignificant to have a separate identity. The wind and the sea beat over it. The rain descends. The sun scorches it. One particle of sand on its own would scarcely be dignified with the title, 'sand' or 'seashore'. Yet, we know that if we lie on the sand and let it trickle through our fingers we discover that its distinctive qualities, which make it sand, depend upon the physical properties of each individual grain of sand. In some ways, a twentieth-century worker, one of 'the masses', can feel that he is nothing but a tiny speck in a gigantic stretch of sand. In the same way, a woman living in a city can often feel that she has no real identity of her own. She is a wife, a mother, another woman among 'women'. We are all susceptible to the feeling that we are just another statistic, taking our identity from other people who control events which affect our lives, almost against our own wishes. It is easy today to find people who share in alienation feelings, like a loss of the sense of purposefulness in life, a crushing sense of the futility of individual action, or a loss of the ability to determine one's own life style. Perhaps at first, when we are young, we are protected from this sense of alienation by our family which gives us our identity, and largely shapes it. At school we absorb some of our character from others, but loneliness begins to be a feature in shaping our adolescence. In young adult life we still hope to force the world around us to take note of us. In middle age most of us have to come to terms with the fact that the world is not going to turn around because of us. At each stage of our lives, because we are human beings and not grains of sand, we are able to reflect on the meaning of the world in which we find ourselves, and we try to discover our own role in life. Just because we are human beings we look beyond our experience and search for a meaning to life. Even if we decide not to think about it at all, we are only capable of that choice because we have first thought and then decided not to admit the thought to our minds. The process of trying to make sense of life is the religious dimension of our lives and is an integral part of ourselves.

Our beliefs, however vague, are important because what we 'are' influences what we do. Some people have personal guide lines but never adopt any formal formula of belief. Others join with those people who have broadly similar beliefs, and then call themselves Hindus, Buddhists, Jews, Christians, Moslems. Our faith is an awareness of our own reality and our relation with forces beyond ourselves. Many of us who have discovered our 'self' in relation to other people and to all creation, become aware of a unity which transcends our separateness. We meet other people, from the past as well as from the present, who seem to be on the same sort of journey. Our pattern of experience interweaves with theirs, and this enables us to communicate the incommunicable.

As a young woman I discovered God through experience. No one was able to tell me about God, nor was I able to get many ideas from books. I learnt first of all through being in touch with myself. I believe that many people share that experience. We come to realise that we are not only the person that other people see. We are not even able to see all of our 'self'. We 'are' because we act, and we act because we 'are'. So we become able to be aware of our elusive 'self'. We can see that 'self' partly through our own eyes and partly through the eyes of others as they reflect our 'self' back to us. There remains a large part of our 'self' of which we are unaware but which nevertheless acts and 'is'. Beyond our own existence as an independent entity, there is the wonder of meeting with other people, with other 'selfs'. Beyond that there is mystery. The atheist rejects the mystery. The religious man accepts the mystery. He sees that all men

G

'are', and supposes that the essence of what they 'are' is rooted in a Unity which gives being to all things. The leap between perceiving that 'you are' and understanding that 'you are because God is', is the leap of faith. No one knows why and how that leap is made by some and not by others.

Having discovered that the experience of the 'self' is important in determining how one actually lives, I, like many others before me, began to explore what it means to 'be'. Now the paradox of this is, that we cannot ever know what it is like to 'be', because when we are there, we 'are', and we cannot therefore experience it. While we are the subject we cannot perceive ourselves as object. We cannot perceive a moment except by moving to the next moment and then looking back. We can only know what has happened by seeing what we have become after the experience is over. When I discovered this I gave up trying to perceive what I was and enjoyed just 'being'. What I have described, is, of course, only one small part of what it means to be a human being. The larger part is concerned with the search for relationship with other people, with creation, and with God, who is within and beyond oneself, within and beyond creation. Because I no longer had to fuss about what I was experiencing, I could get on with the experience. So perhaps I was fortunate enough or perceptive enough to learn something of the meaning of transcendence before I ever came to hear about Transcendental Meditation, and that is why I said to myself, 'Of course, I know what this is about.' In listening to other people struggling to describe what they felt in similar circumstances, and what TM feels like, I have been aware of the absurdity of the exercise. Of course, you can't compare TM with any other experience, because when you are in the fourth state of consciousness you don't know you're there, and so you have no experience with which to compare any other experience. Equally, we can never know what anyone who came to that experience by another route felt. So I could laugh with joy when I came across Jung's insight:

'Every statement about the transcendental is invariably a laughable presumption of the human mind unconscious of its limitations.'[1]

It took me years to discover the truth of that statement for myself. It must have been one of the reasons why Buddha discouraged all theological and metaphysical speculation, but encouraged his disciples to concentrate on the practical problems of living, the elimination of desire and the attainment of 'nirvana'.

In one way it would be quite impossible for me to try to compare my own experience of the state of 'nothingness', or the state of 'being', with the fourth state of consciousness which I would reach through TM. When I am where I am, I do not know what it is like, and when I would be in the fourth state of consciousness I wouldn't know either. What we can all do, it seems to me, is to see whether the effects of prayer in our lives have parallels with the effects of TM in other people's lives. Transcendental Meditation may not be prayer in the Christian sense of the word, but it does have affinities with Christian prayer especially with the prayer of simplicity, and the Maharishi seems to share a common language with mystics from every religious tradition.

Here I have introduced the word 'mystic' for the first time. This word has always eluded definition, but William James, writing at the end of the nineteenth century, gives the best description of the distinctive marks which, when found together, make an experience a mystical one. These marks are that:

1. The experience is indescribable. It has to be directly experienced, but once one has experienced even the beginning of a perception of what lies beyond the here and now, the language used by the mystics becomes understandable.

2. The experience carries a ring of authenticity about it. The mystic is so certain of the reality of it, that he communicates this to others.

3. It is transient, lasting not more than two hours in general.

4. It is passive. The person feels as if he had been taken hold of by some person or force quite outside himself.[2]

I am assuming that mystical experience is a valid experience of people who remain in touch with reality, and are able to live useful social lives. There are scientists who would say that all mystical experience is pathological. I do not, however, find that to be true. What is true, is that mystical experience does not offer proof positive of the existence of God, for such experience is always mediated through the brain and as such it might have a purely psychological basis, as Marghanita Laski claims in her large book on the subject of ecstasy. I personally find this hard to accept for such experiences, repeated many times in many different people, seem so very real. The experience itself is far less important than what God does with and through the mystic, and all the great spiritual writers have emphasised this.

Although, I myself am a middle-aged, robust and busy mother, I have no hesitation in saying that I do understand what the mystics are talking about. The mystical experience is not confined to ascetics in caves nor to celibates. Contemplative awareness is open to everyone. The so-called 'higher' states of mysticism are 'given' experiences which cannot be reached by a person's own effort, so there is no need to worry where one stands on the ladder, nor to think about being a 'special' person, since the gift comes from God and is given to those who need it. I personally think that the 'given' experience is only given for a purpose, a specific individual task, perhaps, which can only be accomplished by some direct contact between God and his agent, but in this I have no certainty, only an intuitive feeling. It has always been a joy to me to find other people with whom I can share this awareness. The poetry of the great mystics is treasured by all the great religious traditions of the world. Each colours his poetry with his own personal touch; that is why we find ourselves more in tune with one writer than with another.

I am going to look at those areas where it seems to me that Transcendental Meditation has its closest affinities with religious prayer. Because the field is so large I shall confine myself mainly to the Hindu and Catholic mystics as they talk about the ordinary ways of prayer which are open to beginners. It should be remembered that the word 'meditation' as used in the East, is the equivalent of the word 'contemplation' as used in the Christian tradition. Before I turn to prayer I want to look at those areas where the mystics of all traditions agree about God and the 'self'.*

POINTS OF AGREEMENT BETWEEN MYSTICS OF ALL TRADITIONS

The nature of the Godhead

All the great mystics of the East and West go beyond an anthropomorphic view of God. They reject any idea that God can be described in human terms, for no idea we have is more than an image of reality. Reality itself can only be 'known' by direct experience. That is why many of the mystics speak in negative terms about God. The great Hindu statement about God: 'God is not this, not that' (Neti, neti), may be compared with the Sufi statement:

> I am not the body
> I am not the senses
> I am not the mind
> I am not this
> I am not that.
> What then am I? What is the self?
> It is in the body
> It is in everybody
> It is everywhere
> It is the All.
> It is self. I am It. Absolute oneness.[3]

* See pages 156–7.

Turning to the Catholic mystics we find the same idea developed by the fifth-century mystic, Dionysius the Areopagite, who was probably a Syrian monk. He may have been in contact with Hindu thought. He wrote a long passage in his treatise on Mystical theology describing God in terms of what He was not. He ends this passage by saying :

'Nor can any affirmation or negation be applied to Him, for although we may affirm or deny the things below Him, we can neither affirm or deny Him, inasmuch as the all-perfect and unique Cause of all things transcends all affirmation, and the simple pre-eminence of His absolute nature is outside of every limitation and beyond them all.'[14]

Ruysbroek describes the Godhead in similar terms :

'The Godhead is in simple essence without activity; Eternal Rest, unconditioned Dark, the Nameless Being, the Superessence of all created things.'[5]

Finally St John of the Cross sums up the mystics' insight :

'We receive this mystical knowledge of God clothed in none of the kinds of images, in none of the sensible representations which our mind makes use of in other circumstances. Accordingly in this knowledge, since the senses and imagination are not employed, we get neither form nor impression, nor can we give any account or furnish any likeness, although the mysterious and sweet tasting wisdom comes here so directly to the innermost parts of the soul.'[6]

The mystics always start from direct experience and draw conclusions about the nature of God based on that experience. This is in contrast to the philosophers who start from a theory about God and then test their hypothesis against observable facts about the universe.

The Unity of everything

The mystics admit of no duality. In Hindu philosophy this oneness of all things extends to good and evil. This can be seen by looking at one of the great religious sculptures of India, the massive stone Trimurti which stands in the caves on Elephant Island, opposite Bombay. The central figure is a three-faced statue, nineteen feet high. The central face is of Brahma, the creator. The left face is of Rudra, the destroyer, and the right face is of Vishnu, the preserver. All three are manifestations of the one God, Shiva. So too the Bhagavad Gita has Krishna saying of himself :

'Among the terrible powers I am the God of destruction.'[7]

Similarly in Chinese thought Tao is the Primal Meaning and Unity behind all creation, but that creation is expressed as the poles of Yang (light) and Yin (darkness). The polarisation between good and evil is central to Christian thought. In relative existence God is not seen to have any part at all in moral evil, although many of the Hebrew prophets see God as the cause of evil, expressed as suffering, pain or disaster.[8] The problem of good and evil has never been resolved satisfactorily in Christian thought, but the mystics sense that good and evil are relative conditions and that beyond them there is a unity. Nicholas of Cusa (15th century) is their spokesman : he taught that in God, seen as superessential unity, all contraries coincide :

'Thus 'tis beyond the coincidence of contradictories that Thou mayest be seen, nowhere this side thereof.'[9]

The real self in union with God

The 'one-ing' of the self and God is the mystic's struggle to describe his experience in non-dualistic terms. The Hindu says, 'The Atman and the Brahman are one : That thou art.' The Christian, St Paul says : 'I live, yet not I but Christ lives in me. It is no longer I who lives but Christ who lives in me.'[10] There are many examples of this kind of thinking among Christian mystics. Meister Eckhart puts it well :

'For the power of the holy Christ seizes the very highest and purest, the spark of the soul, and carries it up in a flame of love . . . the soul spark is conveyed aloft into its source and is absorbed into God and is identified with God and is the spiritual light of God.'[11]

St Teresa of Avila puts it differently using vivid imagery. She speaks of union with God :

'It is as if the ends of two wax candles were joined together so that the light they give is one: the wicks and the wax and the light are all one; yet afterwards the candle can be perfectly well separated from the other and the candles become two again. In spiritual marriage it is like rain falling from the heavens into a river or spring; there is nothing but water there and it is impossible to divide or separate the water belonging to the river from that which fell from heaven.'[12]

The Catholic mystics may describe what union with God feels like but they maintain that there is a distinction between God and the soul. Ruysbroek draws our attention to this:

'Though I have said before that we are all one with God, and this is taught by the Holy Ghost, yet now will I say that we must eternally remain other than God and distinct from Him and this too is taught by Holy Writ. And we must understand and feel both within us if all is to be right with us.'[13]

Julian of Norwich gets round the paradox in this way:

'God is nearer to us than our own soul: for He is the Ground in whom our soul standeth, and He is the mean that keepeth the substance and the sense-nature together so that they shall never dispart. For our soul sitteth in God, in very rest, and our soul is kindly rooted in God in endless love.'[14]

GATEWAYS TO CONTEMPLATIVE AWARENESS
OF GOD

In the Maharishi Mahesh Yogi's descriptions of consciousness, the pilgrim who wishes to attain to union with God must pass through the gateway of Transcendental Meditation. He reaches the fourth state of consciousness and then passes into cosmic consciousness, God consciousness and Union. The Christian pilgrim also travels a road which is somewhat similar. He starts with verbal prayer and reflective meditation and this prayer is often described as prayer of the mind. He moves to a deeper interior silence, in which he becomes aware of the transcendental realities, and this affective prayer is known as the prayer of the heart. He then comes to a gateway which separates what he can achieve alone from what he can only achieve by the grace of God. This is the wordless prayer which has been called acquired contemplation by some, the prayer of simplicity by others, and the prayer of 'loving attention' by St John of the Cross. It is this prayer of simplicity which closely resembles Transcendental Meditation. The mystics give instruction in fair detail for people who are learning to pray with the mind and with the heart. They describe ways of learning to wait attentively on God, of arriving at the gateway to the prayer of simplicity. Beyond this there are no instructions, for God alone is the teacher of those whom He calls to the higher stages of contemplative prayer, whose goal is union.

I have already described in detail the technique of Transcendental Meditation. The prayer of simplicity is widely taught by the mystics of Eastern and Western traditions. Some people use techniques of concentration, using mental or physical exercises which, in themselves, have little value, but they lead the mind to a point from which all the images fall away into stillness. Some people seem to find their way into the prayer of simplicity without any effort at all. Others, and these form the majority, approach this state through the use of 'mantras'. One of the best spiritual guides to this is the author of *The Cloud of Unknowing*. No one else puts it quite so simply as he does:

'Take a short word, preferably of one syllable . . . the shorter the word the better, being more like the meaning of the Spirit: a word like "God" or "love". Choose one which you like, or perhaps some other so long as it is of one syllable. And fix this word fast to your heart, so that it is always there come what may. It will be your shield and spear in peace and war alike. With this word you will hammer the cloud and the darkness above you. With this word you will suppress all thought under the cloud of forgetting.'[15]

Very detailed instructions are given by an Eastern Orthodox writer, the author of *The Way of a Pilgrim*. He uses the Holy Name as a focus:

'Sit down alone and in silence. Lower your head, shut your eyes, breathe out gently and imagine yourself looking into your own heart. As you breathe out say, "Lord Jesus Christ have mercy on me". Say it moving your lips gently, or simply say it in your mind. Try to put all other thoughts aside. Be calm. Be patient and repeat the process frequently.'[16]

Generation after generation of men and women have discovered this way for themselves. They come to a place of darkness, a cloud of unknowing. Here again the language they use to describe this state of being is similar from age to age. For instance, Pseudo-Dionysius tells us:

'Unto this darkness which is beyond light we pray that we may come, and through loss of sight and knowledge may see and know That which transcends sight and knowledge, by the very fact of not seeing and knowing; for this is real sight and knowledge.'[17]

A twentieth-century Benedictine monk describes his prayer time:

'One sets oneself to pray, say for the regulation half hour; empties the mind of all images, ideas, concepts – this is commonly done without much difficulty.

Fixes the soul in loving attention on God, without express or distinct ideas of Him, beyond the vague incomprehensible idea of His Godhead; makes no particular acts but a general actuation of love, without sensible devotion or emotional feelings: a sort of blind and dumb act of the will or of the soul itself. This lasts a few minutes, then fades away, and either a blank or distractions supervene: when recognised, the will again fixes the mind in "loving attention" for a time. The period of prayer is thus passed in such alternations, a few minutes each, the bouts of loving

attention being, in favourable conditions, more prolonged than the bouts of distraction.'[18]

So we see that the reality of this dark state of knowing
is as real to the Catholic mystics as is, the place where
the mind does not exist, but is 'existence' to the
Maharishi.

Turning to the effects of the prayer of simplicity on
the person who prays in this way, we find that the
mystics have as much difficulty in expressing themselves
as do the modern transcendentalists. St Bernard displays
a passionate certainty about the reality of the experience:

'You will ask then, how, since the ways of His access
are thus incapable of being traced, I could know that
He was present? But He is living and full of energy,
and as soon as He has entered into me He has
quickened my sleeping soul, has aroused and softened
and goaded my heart, which was in a state of torpor
and hard as a stone . . . so that my soul might bless
the Lord and all that is within me praise His Holy
Name.'[19]

St Teresa of Avila says to her spiritual daughters:

'If you nevertheless ask how it is possible that the soul
can see and understand that she has been in God,
since during the union she has neither sight nor understanding, I reply that she does not see it then, but that
she does see it more clearly later after she has returned
to herself, not by any vision but by a certitude which
abides in her and which God alone can give.'[20]

I do not think that we can know that the prayer of
simplicity is the same as the Maharishi's fourth state of
consciousness. For one thing we do not have any detailed
studies of the physiological changes in Christian contemplatives at prayer. I do not think that this matters.
They are close. Both are approached through a 'mantra'.
Both require relaxation, with the attention focused inwards, moving to the source of its greatest delight. Both
are indescribable. Yet the mystic and the transcendental-
ist have an inner assurance that each has been at a point
of intersection, and that that experience has profound
effects on one's life after the moment of 'being' has
passed.

The prayer of simplicity is the soul's approach to God.
Metropolitan Anthony reminds us that :

'God who lets us come freely into His presence, is also
free with regard to us . . . He is not bound to reveal
Himself to us simply because we have come and are
gazing in His direction.'[21]

Beyond the gateway of the prayer of simplicity there
are 'given' states of prayer. Some call these higher
states, but the reality is, that, for Christians, they are only
given by God to those whom He calls; and the so-called
higher states of prayer are an intensification of what the
soul had experienced in the prayer of 'loving attention'.
That state radiates out into the whole of the conscious
life of the one who is called to union with God. Again,
the mystics have much to tell us of these states. St Teresa
of Avila writes of deeper states of prayer than most of us
will ever know and yet anyone who has ever slipped into

the prayer of simplicity will understand what she is talking about:

> 'In the orison of union the soul is fully awake as
> regards God, but wholly asleep as regards things of this
> world and in respect of herself. During the short time
> the union lasts, she is, as it were, deprived of every
> feeling and even if she would she could not think of
> any single thing. Thus she needs to employ no artifice
> in order to arrest the use of her understanding: it re-
> mains so stricken with inactivity that she neither
> knows what she loves, nor in what manner she loves,
> nor what she wills. In short she is utterly dead to the
> things of this world and lives solely in God . . . I do
> not know whether in this state she has enough life left
> to breathe. It seems she has not; or at least if she does
> breathe she is unaware of it.'[22]

The Catholic mystics are all clear that their whole lives
become transformed by their direct experience of God in
prayer. Their progress towards God is marked by an increased awareness of the immanence and transcendance
of God at one and the same time. They speak of states
which correspond closely with the Maharishi's higher
states of consciousness, although there are important
differences in Christian and Hindu attitudes towards
these states of prayer which I will be looking at later.
Much of our insight as Christians about Eastern
mysticism has come from Christians who have gone as
missionaries to India and who have adopted the Indian
way of life, and come to a deep understanding of the
Hindu path to God. One Benedictine monk from the

West is now living as a solitary in India and he writes of prayer in a way which Hindu and Christian alike can fully appreciate:

'The spiritual man is anxious to interweave his whole life of prayer with moments of silence; silence during his work and his routine occupations of the day; silence above all during his meditation, whatever form it will take. His silence will first be a silence of the tongue, then silence of the useless thoughts and desires, and finally silence of any thought even the highest. This last and highest silence is the one which has to be sought as often as possible during times assigned to special meditation or contemplation. This silence will be a simple listening to the Spirit within and without, simply being attentive, being aware, being awake.'[23]

At a time when obedience to authority is so much questioned in the world of today, it is startling to meet up with a tiny Indian mystic who demands obedience to a guru as a part of an initiation into Transcendental Meditation. Yet, here again, the Maharishi stands in a tradition which all mystics share.

THE NECESSITY FOR A SPIRITUAL GUIDE ON THE WAY TO GOD

The Vedantists say that one may stumble to a superconsciousness without any previous discipline but that this is not the normal way. The guru, or spiritual master, has always been an important figure in Hinduism and is so

H

for the Maharishi who does not permit his disciples to find their own way into transcendental consciousness, but insists that they be initiated into TM and that they are given the mantra, which has been specially chosen for them by the teacher, to lead them down into the centre of their being. The Catholic mystics are no less insistent upon the need for an experienced guide. In earlier times this need was taken for granted by any serious Christian. People flocked to seek the advice of the desert fathers. Later they abandoned ordinary life in large numbers and sought God through the monastic life of obedience. Obedience to a spiritual director was not only the preroga-aive of the monk or nun. Guides like St Francis de Sales and Père de Caussade were accustomed to directing worldly men and women : and de Caussade, for one, kept a tight rein on his spiritual children. In one of his letters he says :

'In order to be without a director one must have been habitually and for a long time under a director.'[24]

In the Orthodox tradition all this is familiar. There is no nonsense about freedom in the spiritual life for the pilgrim :

'The starets sent me away with his blessing and told me that while learning the prayer I must always come back to him and tell him everything, making a very frank confession and report; for the inward process could not go on successfully without the guidance of a teacher.'[25]

Many of the modern writers do still speak of the neces-

sity for guides along the way, but somewhat *sotto voce*.
The people who have been in long dialogue with the East
are more certain. Abishiktananda says that the path to
the ultimate encounter with the Father in the oneness
of the Holy Spirit is not without its risks :

> 'Nobody should ever engage in it without the help of
> a sure guide – the guru – that is somebody who him-
> self has trodden the path, has been granted at least a
> glimpse of the goal and is prudent enough to lead
> others.'[26]

From reading the Catholic spiritual guides one would
have thought that the direction of souls had always been
one of the most important tasks of the professional priest-
hood and one which priest and people alike would take
for granted. However, there seems to have been some
loss of nerve among all the Western Christian Churches.
As more emphasis has been placed upon the individual
conscience, and upon men's responsibilities for their own
actions, an authority crisis has overtaken all the
Churches. As more emphasis has been placed upon the
need for the social aspects of the Gospel to be proclaimed,
so attention has been withdrawn from the soul's health.
For many Christians in recent times prayer has been a
luxurious extra, rather than an absolute necessity, and
taking time to focus on one's own soul has been seen as
a selfish act. It is not easy to keep the right balance in
life, but it is interesting that prophetic voices are raised
in every Church calling for more teaching in prayer and
contemplation for all men and women of faith. Dom
Aelred Graham speaks for the Roman Catholics :

'Priests of the future, it may be, will learn not only to preside at the Eucharist but to lead the faithful in meditation.'[27]

An Anglican priest, with wide experience of the struggles of young people to find their identity says:

'One of our greatest needs at present is for priests who are concerned primarily with the search for God.'[28]

The need for guides is also recognised by psychiatrists of the standing of R. D. Laing who says:

'Among physicians and priests there should be some who are guides who can educt the person from this world and induct him to the other. To guide him in it and to lead him back again.'[29]

The prophetic voices are not raised in vain. Young people in large numbers have deserted the institutional Churches and crossed denominational barriers in search of spiritual guides who will lead them to truth about themselves, the world in which they live and God. They go where the Spirit leads them, not caring if the search leads to Taizé, or to the Focolare, or to the Maharishi. They are looking for the supernatural to come into their lives and renew it with meaning and joy which they can share with others.

We have to ask why the mystics lay such stress on the need for spiritual guides. Before the middle of the nineteenth century the existence of the spiritual world was accepted. God and the devil were familiar personal beings: the battle between good and evil was fought out in the presence of angels and demons, saints and witches, with powers of extrasensory perception. As science advanced, our knowledge of the natural world also progressed, and many facts attributed to the supernatural came to be understood in terms of physiology and psychology. Men found a reason for the phenomena they saw and lost faith in that which was beyond the phenomena. Science replaced the metaphysical. Priests and prophets were cast aside and many forsook God seeing him as the projection of sick minds. It is only in the last half of this century that scientists have become humble enough to appreciate that the intangible and imperceptible can act in and through the body. Since something so nebulous as stress or anxiety can cause physical change we are less able to be sceptical about faith healing, miracles and paranormal powers. Good and evil have again become real and their effects on men, permanent, tangible and observable. All this has made men more sensitive, and aware that the time is ripe for science and religion to meet again, in the study of that which we cannot see or touch but which is reality. Again, the priest or spiritual man or woman can become skilled in the science of this intangible, imperceptible world which is interpersonal and extra-sensory. The mystic, of all men, knows that in the state of prayer a man is hung suspended between heaven and earth, neither here nor there, neither saved nor damned, and the great spiritual teachers have always said that man is vulnerable in this condition. That is the point at which he needs a guide, a friend, a person who is well acquainted with this state of disassociation, who will protect him from the evil that is outside him and beyond

him, help with the evil that is within him, and lead him
to find wholeness, good and God. Fools and proud men
may venture out on their own, and some will find their
way to God, but more still will lose their way, and some
their reason, if they try to go very far alone.

THE STATE OF BEING AND THE STATE OF PRAYER

I am well aware that in selecting some of the areas where
TM shows affinity to other mystical experiences I
am treading on controversial ground. There are authors,
like Professor R. C. Zaehner, who believe that Catholic
mysticism is unique. The Maharishi himself seems to
imply that his technique of TM is unique, and his followers reiterate the fact that it can be taught to atheist,
agnostic and believer alike, and is not a religious exercise. In describing the ways in which different experiences
are like each other, I am not saying that they are
identical but that they are similar, and may at places
overlap with each other. In the case of TM and prayer,
I am also saying that each can lead to unity which lies
beyond the contraries, the superessential Unity, which
Hindu and Christian alike name God. I have been concerned here to show that TM stands within the mystical
tradition in that it is concerned primarily with the experience of being and of God, rather than with thought
about being and about God. It is a gateway to cosmic
awareness, just as the prayer of simplicity is a gateway
to contemplative awareness. Each point Godwards. Any
man who stands at this intersection can choose to go back,

to stay still, or to go on with the search for wholeness and God.

There are differences between the state of being and the state of prayer. The chief of these is in that fine area which the spiritual teachers call the setting of the will towards God. Whether you are evil or good, you can reach the centre of your being. What you 'are' there, is the sum total of what you have received by inheritance, what you have learnt from life and what you hope to become in the future. These coexist with a general attitude of 'openness', an expectancy which sets the will towards its goal. It is the 'openness' which largely determines what happens to you in the disassociated states of transcendental awareness or the prayer of simplicity. If your will is set towards God, open to the Holy Spirit, then you are likely to find the activity of the Holy Spirit operative in your life, because you have made Him welcome. If your will is set towards yourself, or towards evil, you are likely to find what you set out to look for.

Transcendental Meditation is not prayer. It is something which can exist on its own. I have asked friends who meditate whether they also pray, and many do, recognising the difference intuitively. Some learn to meditate, but then when they are more experienced in prayer, they give it up and continue to pray. I was quite clear, as a young woman, that I had learnt to 'be', before I had any very clear idea of God, incarnate in the person of Christ. Christ gave direction to my being, and the activity of the Holy Spirit united me in prayer to the person of Christ, His Body, the Church. Transcendental Meditation can become a part of prayer, just as the whole of activity can become caught up in prayer. It is the uniting of the will, by intention, with God which is the essence of prayer, and even in the state of union we are told that any person has the free-will to turn his back on God. God does not compel. He draws us to Himself through Love.

I think that for the person who only wants to use TM as a method of deep relaxation, the guide or guru is only necessary while the person is actually learning the technique. Any Hindu, Christian or religious man who is looking beyond that point, needs guidance on the way. The straight road to God has many paths leading off it. We may be tempted to take a short cut by using drugs. We may go too far down a side track and lose our way. We may so easily get so much rest and resurgence of energy from TM that we are tempted to remain in meditation, and so never plod on through the dusty, rather tiresome part of the road that lies ahead in the desert of aridity. Pride may tell us we are at the end of the road when we are just at the beginning. The pitfalls are innumerable. Some people may be led by God directly. Most of us know that it is very hard to distinguish the voice of God from the voice of desire, our 'self', and so we stumble towards God, rather than having the sure confidence that we are on the right road. It is then that signposts, and people who know the way, can be so helpful.

We cannot, I think, treat Transcendental Meditation with scorn, or as a gimmick. It finds a place in scientific experience and in religious experience and bridges the two; yet there are places where the bridge seems a bit weak, the foundations not too firm, and it is with these areas of difficulty that I shall now be concerned.

'By their fruits you shall know them.'

Matthew 7 : 20.

'In all work there may be imperfection
Even as in all fire there is smoke.'

Bhagavad Gita 18 : 48.

6 Some fundamental questions about Transcendental Meditation

When I first became a Christian I found it difficult to find a professional clergyman who would take my intellectual doubts seriously. I remember that I was told that Christianity was a way of life which had to be experienced rather than criticised. Nevertheless, over the succeeding years I have learnt that criticism is part of Christian life. Self-criticism leads us to repentance. Repentance for sin is an integral part of our Christian discipline, and yet our penitence should always be set within a context of growth. Christ draws us into Love as we grow away from ourselves, and from sin, towards him and our neighbour. Whatever applies to the individual applies equally to the community of which we are a part. We are all used to hearing the Church criticised and we know that there are many areas where there is a real need for reform. As Christians we are so used to serious criticism from inside the Church, as well as from people outside it, that, on the whole, we now answer doubts with the attention they deserve.

My memories of my intellectual struggles, when I first joined the Church, revived when I came to meet TM enthusiasts for the first time. Among them the spirit of

self-appraisal, and any critical evaluation of the technique of TM, seemed almost non-existent. Morale being
high, it was not easy to find dissidents within the movement. Even creative criticisms were apt to be dismissed,
with the assurance that once you became an initiate all
your questionings would disappear. On occasion I was
faced by such apparent naïvety and indifference to the
real problems and sufferings of the world, that I found it
required some determination to go deeper into the claims
of Transcendental Meditation. However, I persisted, for
real dialogue can be very helpful if people with opposite
views can stay with each other and really explore their
points of difference. This chapter explores those areas in
which I have found it difficult to reconcile my Christian
point of view with that of TM, or my medical knowledge
with the assertions made about TM.

RELIGIOUS QUESTIONS

There are two obvious theological differences between the
tradition in which the Maharishi's teaching is rooted and
the tradition in which the Christian stands. All mystics
perceive the unity of the Godhead, the original Source
of all creation, in the same way. They differ in their concepts about the person of God. The Maharishi, like many
Hindus, accepts Christ as one of the incarnations of God.
He emphasises that TM is not prayer, not a religion, and
that the fourth state of consciousness is achieved effortlessly, as easily by the atheist as by the devout Hindu,
Buddhist or Christian. It can be reached by man's desire
alone.

The Christian tradition, on the other hand, is incarnational and Christocentric. All Christian thought is Christ centred, and He is seen as the one Incarnate God through whom salvation is assured. The mystics do not always articulate this very clearly, because they are describing what happens to them in prayer. They are describing an experience not stating their beliefs. This fact has made many mystics suspect. St John of the Cross has been accused of being more of a Buddhist than a Christian on occasion. However, he effectively disposes of this accusation :

'For in giving us, as He did, His son which is His Word – and He has no other – He spake to us all together, once and for all in this single Word, and He has no occasion to speak further . . . Wherefore he that would now enquire of God, or seek any vision or revelation, would not only be acting foolishly, but would be committing an offence against God, by not setting his eyes altogether upon Christ, and seeking no new thing or aught beside. For He is my complete speech and answer, and He is my vision and my revelation.'[1]

In the past, Christians have found it difficult to regard religions like Hinduism as being able to contain Truth. Everything necessary to salvation lay within the Christian Church and one did not need to look elsewhere. Changing conditions have made it necessary to understand one another, and the Catholic Church is now welcoming inter-denominational cooperation. Many Christians have been led to the discovery of the hidden Christ in Hinduism, just as they have been able to incorporate Zen into Catholicism. The fact that the Maharishi Mahesh Yogi does not believe that Christ is his personal saviour, need not prevent any Christian from creative encounter with TM.

The second great difference between the Maharishi's tradition and the Christian one, is that in Hinduism there is no Holy Spirit. A man can attain to his ultimate end by a gradual process of self-evolution. There is no go-between for the Hindu, no prompting by the Breath of God towards transcendance. The mystery is taken out of awareness. In his presentation of the Science of Creative Intelligence the Maharishi seems to concentrate on promoting TM as an expedient solution to a number of problems, of which the chief is stress. The absence of any sense of dependence on God's initiative takes away any need for humility on the part of the seeker. Humility is the foundation of the Christian spiritual life; it is lacking in the Maharishi's teaching as it appears in SCI.

All Christians would accept that they are not the masters of their fate nor the captains of their souls. They are dependent on God. Christians know that there are many routes by which people can reach God, but they state that in all cases it is the leading of the Spirit which leads to truth, even where the name of Christ goes un-recognised. This enables Christians to see that people have different gifts, different temperaments and different op-portunities to use their talents. All the great spiritual directors have a very flexible approach to an individual's approach to God. The right way for one person might not be the right way for another. Each person has gifts which cannot be compared with any other person's gifts. Each has a duty to use those gifts, and develp them according to God's will, but some people may be active, some contemplative, some imaginative, some creative, some pedestrian. All are part of the body and there is no one way which is right for all. A Christian, because of his dependence on God, could not say that a man must follow only one particular way of meditation if he is to find the right path to God. The Christian could not say that thinking and feeling are less important than the surrender of those faculties in order to 'be'. The Christian would feel that Being could find its true expression as much in activity as in stillness, as much in passion as in withdrawal, as much in stress as in relaxation.

The problem of evil

The Maharishi is quite definite in saying that all stress is harmful and all suffering unnecessary. He pays little attention to the problem of evil, and to the suffering of the world, except to say that all the methods, which men use to try to solve the problems which confront them, are less efficient than his simple solution that everyone should meditate. He leaves the impression that TM is a panacea for all the world's ills, and that all men who meditate will naturally tend to good and so will bring in the kingdom of God upon earth. It has always been difficult for utopians to realise that all men are not as good as they would like to be. Man has selfish capacities within himself which are as powerful as his capacity for selflessness. The Christian religion may have paid too great an attention to the dark side of man's nature, and to the evil forces which surround him; but evil does not disappear simply because we refuse to think about it. The Maharishi is splendidly practical when he tells us that the best way to overcome darkness is to turn on the light, rather than trying to grope through the darkness to find out why it is so dark. He points the way towards positive thinking about perfect love casting out fear, but at times he oversimplifies. In effect, he says that the contact with Being, through the experience of TM, will automatically make you a 'good' sort of a person. On the other hand, Christianity teaches that you usually have to want to be good to be able to contact Being (God) in the first place, though it is God who inspires you to want to reach him. A Christian expects to do battle with sin all through his life. We know for a fact that both these insights can be true. St Paul was converted by direct contact with Christ. At the same time he recognised the darkness of his own nature. Christian contemplatives down the ages witness to the fact that prayer of itself does not automatically cure you of your tendency to sin, nor of the necessity to come to terms with the evil side of your own nature.

One of the great unsolved questions which I find about TM is the comparative lack of teaching about evil. I can appreciate that in Hindu philosophy the principles of 'karma' and 'maya' make relative existence, and its evils, less important than absolute Being. Yet, for me, relative existence is as important and as real as transcendence. Relative existence is part of absolute reality. The forces of real evil are engaged in battle with the forces of good within the soul and within creation.

When a Christian begins to pray he often finds it a joyful experience. There comes a time for nearly all of us when it becomes hard to pray. Aridity descends. Our own passions rise up to confront us and threaten us. Sitting down to pray becomes the signal for distraction, delusion, illusion and turbulence. The Maharishi's people to whom I have spoken do not appear to know any of this. According to them, their 'mantra' carries them safely and surely to the centre of their being, and their contact with Being leads them on to greater internal harmony, which leads naturally to their becoming morally good. It is difficult to see how a man is to tackle his own nature if he remains so unaware of his capacity for evil. Simply by observing the behaviour of men and women in ordinary life situations we must conclude that people are a mixture of good and evil. The behaviour of people springs from what they are. A man who meditates does not discard his own personality but takes it with him into the nothingness of being. None of us likes to face the evil that is within us. We tend to project on to God only those qualities which we think that He should possess. We have to ask ourselves whether thinking of the Absolute only in terms of moral good is realistic. Perhaps the Jews were wise when they portrayed their God as so involved in men's affairs that He was angry, punitive and revengeful on occasions. Perhaps our image of our Christian God has become too good to be real to anyone. We reduce the humanity of Christ if we only see Him as a meek and gentle man. He must have had a capacity to be tempted while remaining without sin. The joy of being fully human is that we are capable of good and evil. We know that even the evil side of ourselves can be harnessed and used creatively once we recognise it, accept it, and submit it to God. Our own capacity for evil is distasteful to us, and it becomes easy to deceive ourselves; but the

I

emphasis on moral teaching, which is found in Christianity, constantly reminds us of our ability to sin, and this gives us a chance to become sensitive to ourselves.

In practice, a lack of moral teaching can lead to the sort of hedonism which rejoices in meditation without our perceiving the effect of our behaviour on other people. This is a hazard for Christian contemplative and Transcendental Meditator alike. I have had personal experience of intense enthusiasts from both disciplines who come to visit. They insist on having their meditation time while you wash up, cook the dinner and try to keep the children quiet so as not to disturb them. They rejoice in their increased energy, while you wilt with tiredness. They tell you about the joy and peace they feel, while you struggle with the pain of knowing that you want to hit them for being so self-satisfied, and unaware of the inconvenience they have caused around them. Of course, it is easy to be critical and to exaggerate, but what I have said can be true, unless those who adopt contemplation or meditation are careful to balance silent withdrawal with outward activity which is rooted in Love. Christian spirituality constantly emphasises this teaching, but Hindu and Christian alike can become obsessed with their own salvation, and indifferent to the plight of other people and to evil within the community. The Christian contemplative, Daniel Berrigan, reminds us of these dangers :

'In a time when a machine is claiming its victories over men and women it seems to me that contemplation becomes a form of resistence and should lead to resistance in the world . . . I mention this because this also is not

clear, and in the derangement of our culture we see
that people move towards contemplation *in despair* –
even though unrecognised. *They meditate as a way of
becoming neutral* – to put a guard between themselves and the horror around them, instead of allowing
them to give themselves to people and to hope,
instead of presenting something new to suffering
people. We have a terrible kind of drug called
'contemplation'. The practitioners may call themselves Jesus freaks or followers of Krishna or Buddha;
they may wear robes of some kind, be in the street and
beg and pray and live in communes, but they care
nothing about the war. *Nothing about the war.* And
they talk somewhat like Billy Graham : "Jesus saves";
that is they say : "it's not necessary to do anything".
So they become another resource of the culture instead of a resource against the culture.'[2]

These words were written by a man who believes that his
actions spring out of contemplation. Along with others,
he believed it to be right to commit a technically
criminal action because he could no longer remain silent
or passive in the face of the suffering he saw in Vietnam,
and he protested as an individual on behalf of his fellow
men.

This passage highlights some of the difficulties which
face the people who draw apart from life in order to
meditate or to pray. Contact with the Absolute, with
God, is itself an experience which changes you. It does
not automatically make you good and therefore concerned with the evils of the world. It was after he became
a Christian that St Paul wrote :

'The good that I want to do, I fail to do; but what I do is the wrong which is against my will; and if what I do is against my will, clearly it is no longer I who am the agent but sin that has its lodgings in me.'[3]

St Paul knew the strength of his own evil nature. Yet he believed that it could be redeemed by the person of Christ who had died for him, and yet was alive within him. Christians of today know the truth of this paradox.

Christians also know the capacity of evil to mimic good. They, therefore, feel that they must test their spiritual experiences against the person of Jesus Christ, as revealed in Scripture. They are also guided by the doctrines and traditions of their own Church.

The Maharishi Mahesh Yogi relies on the contact with the Absolute, through Transcendental Meditation, to achieve goodness. He teaches that goodness must follow TM and does not rely on any one moral code, although his books contain teaching about the art of gracious living. Such a powerful technique as TM should not be given to the world without some concern about how it is used. The Maharishi is confident that the technique will only produce good people. He is so confident of this that he happily teaches soldiers the method, believing that in time the method will modify the soldiers' attitude to war. Everyone will sincerely hope that in this his confidence will be fulfilled; yet it is known that comparable techniques, like Zen, were used by the Nazis for the effects they had on energy and well-being. The fact that you set out to meet Being, and that you transcend consciousness, does not necessarily guarantee that you meet Absolute good so that you are transformed by It into the image of God. That is sad reality, for the Christian at any rate, and it can only be the result of the known capacity for evil, 'the sin that has its lodging in me'.

All who set out on the journey towards God know that there are perils on the way. Some of them are of our own making. Among these are pride, self-absorption, spiritual gluttony, and contempt for others. These are the special dangers of contemplatives. There are also the evils which befall us through the jealousies and antagonisms of others. The followers of Christ accept that suffering will be part of their vocation, for they challenge the consciences of other men. Hostility and ridicule have to be endured by many who learn to pray. Even persecution and martyrdom can be the consequence of becoming a Christian. These outside hatreds and evils have to be transformed in love, through Love. The Christian faces evil and overcomes it in himself. The follower of the Maharishi is more likely to pass through it without noticing. Both are valid ways to God, but they are different; and the Christian who meditates for the joy and sense of well-being that he gains will do well to remember that meditation is not enough in itself. It must be balanced by prayer and activity if the whole of one's life is to be given to the service of God.

I have not yet met any of the Maharishi's followers who have any intimate knowledge of the force of evil. This may be because I am unlikely to have met any of his followers who have gained cosmic or God consciousness, or it may be because I am an outsider. The Maharishi himself speaks little of these forces. Many Christian contemplatives, however, will know the force of the evil which is in them as it reverberates in tune with the collective evil of mankind and with absolute evil. The disassociated state which accompanies the prayer of simplicity 'opens' the eye of the soul to the dark cloud of unknowing. The prayerful man becomes sensitive to a greater degree than the man who never prays in this way. This is probably why the mystics have often been people with paranormal powers of perception, awareness and even prediction. These paranormal powers are incidental. They need not exist, but often do, and are yet another hazard in the spiritual life. A man or woman with extrasensory perception can often see the problems which beset others very clearly and can, as it were, tune into the other person's subconscious mind. Many have the spiritual gifts of prophecy, foreknowledge, and healing. These gifts are sometimes given for the good of the community where they can be used in cooperation with the Holy Spirit for the greater glory of God. They can equally well be used for self-glorification and for gaining power over other people's lives.

TRANSCENDENTAL MEDITATION AND THE COMMUNITY

A Christian is protected from himself to some extent because he lives his life in a community of people with the aid of the Word of God and the sacraments of the Church. He can, therefore, keep a proper sense of proportion about his life and is subject to the discipline of the common life. If he is wise and humble the contemplative will submit himself to the overall direction of a

trusted guide. Every Christian should be able to rejoice
that he lives in this community. Unfortunately there is
ample evidence that many Christians today do not find
the kind of strength and love within their own community which they need, and so they turn to other disciplines which they think will give them what is missing.
The fact that thousands of thinking and sensitive people
are turning away from the Church to look for this sort of
fellowship is a judgement on the institutional Church.
We cannot be content to say that the Holy Spirit is at
work outside the structures of the Church. He is both outside and inside, but we should pray that He may become
visible at all times within the community of the Body of
Christ. The Spiritual Regeneration Movement is not a
community. Transcendental Meditation is not a sacra-
ment of fellowship but a technique for the individual.
Common life is not the essence of the SRM as it is of the
Christian community. It is true that the Mararishi has
such charisma that the people close to him probably do
constitute a community: but it is less likely that that kind
of fellowship is so closely experienced by the person who
learns meditation in order to free himself from tension.
The synthesis between immanence and transcendence
does take place in the higher states of consciousness in
the Maharishi's scheme of things but it is still rather a
solitary synthesis. In the last two or three years the SRM
has cast off its semi-religious clothing and has pursued
science in a big way. It will be a pity if the technique
undergoes a process of secularisation in which the transcendent becomes banal.

MEDICAL QUESTIONS

The problem of suffering

The Maharishi states that stress should give way to
relaxation, and sees suffering as a destructive and
unnecessary evil. We have to look at the problem of suffering and decide whether it is always bad, never to be
tolerated, or whether it can help us towards growth. For
many hundreds of years Christians and others have met
suffering by accepting its inevitability. We find ourselves caught up in it and often try to cope with it by
transcending it. We know it is here. We feel its effects.
We try to go beyond it, rise up above it, achieve what we
want to despite it. The Cross is central to Christian
thought and the Resurrection doesn't make sense without the Incarnation and the crucifixion. Christians look
to find resurrection through suffering and death. The
total removal of suffering from our lives might not be as
good for us as we should like to think. Suffering is a part
of life and anything which removes it from consideration
as a part of creation tends to a lopsided view of wholeness.

In saying that suffering is part of life, I am not saying,
either that it should be sought or that it should go un-
relieved in individual circumstances. I am saying that it
can be creative. Many of my patients seem to feel that
they will only be 'normal' if they never feel any pain,
never feel anxious or depressed. They sometimes come to
ask for relief from the normal stress of life, and within a
total context of wholeness I do not believe that what they

are asking for is normal or desirable. On the other hand, my whole life is spent in trying to relieve suffering where it becomes intolerable or excessive. While I believe that mental anguish should always be relieved when it threatens a person with incapacity, I should be chary of reducing stress and suffering to the point where they are no longer a factor in creativity and growth. For instance, we know that in everyday experience a moderate degree of tension helps us to accomplish something we want to do, better than if we were so relaxed that we didn't care about the outcome of our action. If you face an exam, an interview for a job, or a challenge of any sort you don't want to be so relaxed that you sink into an apathetic state. If you do, you are not very likely to do well. Being moderately nervous often helps a person to produce his best effort for a particular occasion. Anyone who has ever prepared a public speech will know how difficult it is to get the feel of the speech during rehearsal. It is only under the stimulus of the audience that the speaker really comes alive. At a more creative level, we know that many of the great writers and artists have written and painted from life situations of great personal hardship and un-happiness. The same is true of musicians; Beethoven provides an excellent example. The Maharishi's English disciples to whom I have spoken say that no one can tell what Beethoven might have accomplished had he not been under stress. This may be true, but it seems to me to be too simplistic an answer. It is, surely, a question of degree; and where stress and tension can be reduced without a loss of perspective we may rejoice. I do not accept that suffering is always bad. Pain and physical discomfort often warn us of disease which would otherwise go unsuspected. Mental tension can help us to pay attention to the way in which we live our lives. Our own suffering can help us to become more sensitive to the sufferings of other people. The fact is that as human beings we are a delicate amalgam of many parts. We can only exert partial control over our environment and we are constantly having to adapt in order to survive. It is where we fail to adapt, or the outside stress is so great that we are flooded with it, that we break down under the strain and become ill.

I still hold that TM is very valuable in building up our inner resources of strength. Just because TM is for all and not only for the recluse, we are able to reach a balance between relaxation and effort. If we keep the thing in proportion we shall probably find ourselves meditating for only two half hour periods a day. The rest of the day is spent in normal activity. It is wrong to think of TM as a kind of defence system, to keep stress out. In fact the person who meditates absorbs stress but is then able to release it through meditation so that it does not build up inside the body and cause damage. This, indeed, is how most people actually see TM. As with all techniques, it can be misused.

PRACTICAL PROBLEMS

Christians who meet TM have to ask themselves: 'Is this for me'? There are some practical difficulties which may get in the way of a good technique. One of the chief of these difficulties is the rightness of a Christian becoming involved with an initiation ceremony. The Maharishi's followers have told me that this presents little difficulty in practice. They explain that the pupil does not have to participate actively, but only be present at the ceremony. They say that very few people dislike it. However, several practising Christians have found it difficult, particularly as it is not at present an optional alternative but mandatory if you want to learn TM. Perhaps the best way round this difficulty is to see it as a thanksgiving for the long tradition of wisdom which can produce such jewels as the Bhagavad Gita. Any Christian must feel that that is worth being thankful for. I personally remember the time when Roman Catholics could not participate in the Christian worship of other denominations, let alone take part in any act of worship which was non-Christian. This particular difficulty may be a 'hangover' from my own youth for it certainly does not appear to bother many of the young people who take it up.

A second important practical difficulty is the use of a Sanskrit 'mantra'. We shall avoid this difficulty if we understand that TM is not a prayer but a technique for deep relaxation and rest. The difficulty here is psychological. TM has such close affinities with the prayer of simplicity, and the Christian is familiar with the use of Christian 'mantras' so that the two exercises become easily mixed up with each other. Faced with this problem I have to ask myself how much it really matters? The essence of Christian thought is that God is present everywhere and at all times. There is never a time when God is not present even though at times we feel that we are separate from Him. It cannot really matter if we turn relaxation into prayer or make prayer a relaxation. Prayer is a relationship with God and we do not always have to make a deliberate conscious effort to be aware of God. Prayer is a relationship which permeates the whole of our lives, and although we use formal times of prayer to recollect ourselves in the presence of God, He is no less present in every activity of the day. The quibble about the use of non-Christian 'mantras' can be seen in proportion only if we have a wide understanding of the meaning of prayer as a relationship. Probably most of the difficulty which we have here is that we love the familiar Christian 'mantras' and are unwilling to substitute anything for the Name of Jesus. Undoubtedly it would be helpful to sincere Christians if they were able to omit the initiation ceremony and also to use meaningful Christian 'mantras'. At least one person known to me has substituted a Christian 'mantra' for the given Sanskrit one, and apparently learnt the technique to the satisfaction of the teacher who never knew what his pupil had done. Of course, we have to remember that any Christian 'mantra' only carries meaning at the beginning of the prayer of simplicity, which leads quickly into the 'cloud of unknowing'.

It seems to me that TM should be adaptable enough to take in these reservations of religious people, but equally perhaps religious people can be adaptable without feeling that they are betraying their faith.

Another purely practical problem for the practising Christian is the time factor. We naturally spend time at the Eucharist and in prayer. On top of this many of us read the scriptures and other devotional books every day, and if we are going to add an hour to the daily routine we are going to have to crowd other activities out. On the other hand, many of us indulge in frenetic activity and good works out of a sense of guilt lest we become selfish in spending time on ourselves. It is perhaps the people who are really busy who most need to rid themselves of stress. I have certainly found this to be true in my own life. If I press on with activity when I am tired and tense the activity suffers and I suffer. If I learn to relax then I am refreshed and my subsequent activity is more easily accomplished and more efficient. Here again it is a question of degree and of living a balanced life. It is so important if we are busy people to be relaxed so that we are not felt by others to be rushed. Business is very exhausting and off-putting to other people, often the very people towards whom we have responsibility. It seems to be an occupational hazard of Christians to hurry through life from one activity to another; it is certainly an occupational hazard of people like priests, doctors, social workers, mothers. There is so much to be done, and apparently so little time to do it, that one spends no time at all with the people who are with us, because we are too busy thinking of the next person or the next activity ahead of us. TM can have a real value in a rule of life in that it enables us to focus on relaxation and then that restfulness can carry over into the rest of our living.

I should like to end this chapter on the problems which have to be faced by a serious enquirer about TM with a plea for a wider appreciation of its proper use in individual life.

TM is not the only method by which we can release stress. It is a good way. There are others. People are not all of the same temperament. Many find it more relaxing to sink themselves into rhythmic exercise or to lose themselves in beautiful music or an absorbing book. The time when we most need to fall back on a good technique is when we have lost the knack of spontaneous relaxation. When this happens we are in trouble. We sit down, but cannot concentrate. We find that we are restless and light a cigarette or pour ourselves a drink. Sometimes our legs get jerky or our muscles twitch. At other times we may notice that our fists are clenched. Our thoughts interrupt the flow of music or intrude upon the pages of a book. Everyone who takes the trouble to notice what is going on in himself can learn the clues which tell him that he is under stress and no longer coping efficiently with it. The trouble is that so often we blind ourselves to the clues. We do not want to think of ourselves as vulnerable and so we often pretend that if we ignore the symptoms they will go away. This is called, 'working it out of our system': what it really means, is that we work the stress into the system until eventually the whole system collapses under the strain. The technique of TM is simple and it works. Once we have learnt it we can easily recover the method, even if we have given it up for a time. While it would be foolish to ignore the spiritual dangers of TM, or of prayer for that matter, it would be foolish to reject its benefits. I would say that the religious man, whether he be Hindu or Christian, has the sort of stability and purpose in life which should enable him to make the best use of a technique like Transcendental Meditation. The religious man sees himself always in relationship with God, his environment and his neighbours. He is always in interaction, and appreciates that not only does he influence his environment, but also is influenced by it, and that, 'all things work together for good to them that love God'.[4]

It would be sad to see TM used as a panacea for stress conditions, or as an end in itself, with pleasure and self-advancement as the only goals. I am glad if pleasure and a sense of well-being enable men to serve the world better, and I think that TM has a valuable part to play within the world.

'This is my commandment :
    Love one another,
    As I have loved you.'

               John 15 : 12.

'Only by love can a man
See me and know me
    And come unto me.'

           Bhagavad Gita 11 : 54.

7 The way ahead.
Transcendental Meditation and the world.

Transcendental Meditation is significant for many people because of its immediate effects on their lives. They feel better. They are happier. They have more energy. They become more balanced people and are able to rediscover a sense of purpose to life. Some may become aware of a mystery in life of which they were previously unaware. Some may even rediscover religious awareness.

The effects of TM on individual lives are important. No one could deny that, especially if they had met someone who had been rescued from dependence on 'hard' drugs by the technique. Yet Transcendental Meditation has a still greater significance. It is a meeting point between religion and science. It is also a meeting point for people of different faiths. Both these meeting points could result in real encounter to the benefit of the whole world.

At one time religion dominated observed fact. If observed fact didn't fit into religious theories about God and the world, then observed fact had to be suppressed or refuted. Galileo was one of the victims of this sort of thinking. Moreover, observed fact demanded a spiritual explanation. Again in the Western world this was worked out in concrete terms. Mentally sick people were thought to be 'possessed'. They were tortured and killed as witches. All this was done from the best motives and because of inadequate scientific knowledge. God gave men minds to use, and in the course of time science enabled men to refute some misconceptions about life and to discover many new facts about God's creation. For a time reason came to dominate the world and sometimes appeared to provide irrefutable evidence that much of the old religious teaching was wrong in its facts and misguided in its conclusions. Science was seen as a contradiction of religion, and observed fact carried no deeper meaning that pointed beyond the natural to a supernatural Cause. Self advancement and enlightened humanism became the chief principles which dominated the behaviour of individuals in the Western hemisphere. The other peoples of the world were considered to be in neeed of enlightenment and liberation from their heathen superstitions, presumably so that they could become subject to Western materialism. However, God does not die so easily, and now we stand at a point of time where many scientists are beginning to meet with a mystery which doesn't fit into their explantions, and men everywhere are beginning to look with horror at the sort of world they are creating for their children. There are in fact all sorts of signposts to show that this sort of rethinking is taking place among scientists and there are all sorts of frontiers where there is now serious dialogue and co-operation between scientists and men of faith.

Jung was one of the foremost explorers of the mind and his theories about the collective unconscious are well known. About the time that he was propounding his theories, other scientists, like Fliess of Berlin, Swoboda of Vienna, and Professor Teltscher in Austria, were exploring the rhythms which control much of men's lives. The science of biorhythmics came into being and studies have been going on ever since. They show the existence of definite rhythms in the physical, emotional and intellectual spheres of life. These cycles recur at twenty-three, twenty-eight and thirty-three days respectively, and interact with other known rhythms of life, such as the diurnal cycle and the menstrual cycle. Many of the 'old wives tales' were shown to have a scientific basis and it has become impossible to dismiss, as superstition, ideas which people have about certain days in their lives being bad ones or unlucky. 'Critical' days do occur, as the Japanese have shown in a study of pilot errors in air accidents, when they demonstarted that accidents were twice as likely to occur when the pilot was in a critical phase of his periodic rhythm, that is, all his functions were at their nadir. 'Bad' days can now be predicted with a fair degree of certainty. 'Moon madness' no longer seems so ridiculous as it did twenty or thirty years ago. It is no longer possible for men to point to the emotional instability of women at the time of their menstrual periods and think themselves immune from cyclical variations of well-being, mood and intellectual ability. The external manifestations are not so apparent: that is all.

In addition, we now have good evidence about the biological time clocks which govern the behaviour of animals and influence that of men, and we have evidence about the ill effects of interfering with these circadian rhythms of individuals. Animals subject to assault of their rhythms have been known to develop malignant tumours, whereas the controls, whose natural rhythms were left untouched, did not.

Scientists can no longer laugh at extrasensory perception, or the ability of a man's mind to affect solid matter. The researches into paranormal phenomena, reported by people like Renée Haynes, Koestler and Lyall Watson, leave us in no doubt about the fluidity of matter and its sensitivity to thought waves, even at considerable distance. Faith healing becomes intelligible as scientific fact, and it need no longer be relegated to the realms of naïve religious credulity. In former times, scientists used to reject anything they could not accurately observe and classify. Now, scientists are increasingly exploring areas of life which formerly would have been considered to be the province of theologians. Twenty years ago it was rare to find a weighty scientific paper on a subject like meditation. Now they proliferate, and meditation is taken seriously, thanks to the collaboration between a Hindu guru and scientists from many countries. TM is one of the frontier areas where scientists are coming into contact with the mystery of being and with areas of the human mind which are, as yet, little explored. There is now ample proof that the unseeable, immeasurable forces at the centre of being are producing measurable physical effects, and, in some cases, are producing permanent change.

The religious man has no need to fear this incursion of science into his territory. That is one lesson which the Maharishi gives us. It is true that the dogmas of the institutional Church are still under attack, but experience of the areas of life which we cannot explain has increased many people's faith rather than diminished it. None of us can prove the existence of God at the centre of our being but we do know that what we are and what we believe has profound and measurable effects on the matter of which the universe consists.

Science is ripe for reunion with religion and all bridge-heads between the two are to be welcomed. It is, after all, absolute truth which we all seek, not the wishful thinking that has passed for truth in the past. That is why Transcendental Meditation is more important than the sum total of its effects on individual lives. It is a signpost for the future.

THE IMPORTANCE OF TRANSCENDENTAL MEDITATION FOR RELIGION

The Maharishi would be the first to admit that he is not teaching anything new. He has brought out insights which have been known to Hindus for hundreds of years and has made them available to all. He has presented the technique of TM in a new way, and has taught that the method is available to all people and is not reserved for those who are travelling on the path of renunciation. This is new, and because it is new, and because the Maharishi has gone out to look for men instead of waiting for them to come to him, he is out of favour with some of his own compatriots. It is interesting to note that it is only in recent times that the Catholic Church has taught that the religious life is not a higher way of life than the married state but a different vocation within the whole body of the Church. Baptism is more important than either. Only recently has it been accepted that contemplation is open to all whom God calls.

One of the most controversial aspects of the

Maharishi's teaching has been that no special prepara-
tion is necessary before you can meditate. Anyone can
meditate, provided that he is ready to be taught in the
approved way. It may be rather annoying, if you have
been trying to find God through complicated yoga techniques, to be told that you need not have gone through
all that self discipline in order to find Him at the centre
of your being. The refreshing simplicity of the Maharishi's
teaching is another signpost for religious people.
Christians, too, have studied the psychology of asceticism
and are now coming to simplicity of life, and a deep appreciation of the discipline which Love evokes, which
makes harshness towards the self less necessary.

Transcendental Meditation is a signpost for the
Christian Church in pointing out the large number of
young people who want to search for meaning in their
lives, and who are prepared to sit down and learn what
being fully human means. Meditation explores the
mystery of being at first hand. That is what people want
to learn about. Dogma is less important than experience
in determining how you actually live, and the Maharishi's
insistence on the value of meditational experience in
forming character is of importance to the institutional
church which has traditionally placed a lot of emphasis
on moral instruction.

The sheer professionalism of the Maharishi's teachers
is welcome. He trains his teachers thoroughly and well.
They do not have to maintain buildings and administer
organisations as well as teach meditation, although many
of them do have to earn their own living. They get ex-
penses only for their work for the SRM. The Christian
Church might do well if it concentrated some of its re-

sources on training spiritual guides, who would have no other responsibilities than the spiritual formation of men and women who sought God. People want to learn to pray and they want to be taught properly. It is an open question as to whether this teaching should be discursive, authoritative, or individual, for people vary greatly in their attraits. On the other hand, simple techniques, like the Jesus prayer, and yoga breath control, and contemplative postures, can and should be well taught. There is no lack of men and women, priests or laity, who could learn to be teachers of prayer. While the Church refuses to take the demands of people seriously, they will leave her in increasing numbers to try to find what they are looking for from anyone who is willing to teach them. Maybe it does require humility to learn from a Hindu monk, but I cannot think that it would do anyone any harm, given a firm faith and a strong sense of community.

Some Western monks have gone to the East and tried to find the Christ in India by trying to assimilate the Indian way of life to their Christian monasticism. Their hope is that Hindus will also learn from them about the Christ, and will find Him within the Hindu way of life. These ventures have been well described. In the West a Hindu guru has come to teach us about his insights for the world. He burns with enthusiasm for his message to the world, and proclaims it unashamedly wherever the doors are opened to him. He says that he cares what happens to the world. Christians would say the same. Together they witness to an alternative way of living. Together they proclaim that there is more to living than the acquisition of material wealth, and the gaining of power over other people's lives. The Maharishi is a partner to all religious men who bear witness to the values of human life. We do well to value his witness highly. I will end with some words from Thomas Merton, which describe men like the Maharishi Mahesh Yogi :

'The man who has attained final integration is no longer limited by the culture in which he has grown up. He does not remain bound to one limited set of values in such a way that he opposes them aggressively or defensively to others. He has a unified vision and experience of the one truth shining out of all the various manifestations : some clearer than others, some more definite and certain than others . . . With this view of life he is able to bring perspective, liberty and spontaneity into the lives of others.'[1]

Discussion: Transcendental Meditation

Members of the editorial board of *Theoria to theory* (collectively called 'Questioner') talk with Una Kroll, Anthony Campbell and John Windsor.

This discussion arose out of an article entitled 'The Dangers of Meditation' by Una Kroll in The Times *of June 30th 1973 in which she drew attention to some striking affinities between descriptions of states of consciousness in Transcendental Meditation and states experienced by Christian and Buddhist contemplatives. She also said that too little attention was paid by teachers of TM to the dangers in altered states of consciousness, of which religious teachers were so aware, and queried the wisdom of separating TM from a religious way of life. John Windsor wrote a letter challenging Una Kroll's article, describing it as 'hostile' because of the comparison she drew between changes in consciousness which occur during TM and drug induced changes, which she said could lead to murder and suicide. He said that the comparison was unsupported. We invited them to come and continue the discussion with us. We also invited Anthony Campbell, having read his book* Seven States of Consciousness. *Anthony Campbell and Una Kroll are both doctors.*

'Transcendental Meditation' is the name given by Maharishi Mahesh Yogi, the Indian monk and teacher, to his technique in tapping the innate ability of the nervous system to rid itself of stress and fatigue effortlessly and at will. When learning the technique, each would-be meditator is given a mantra – the thought of a sound devoid of meaning – which is used in a specified way. Maharishi defines the mantra as 'the vehicle for the natural tendency of the mind to ride on'.

U.K. I should like to begin by saying that contrary to the impression I seem to have left with John Windsor, judging by his comments on my *Times* article on the subject of TM, I am not 'hostile' to TM. I would however, like to clarify some of the issues which raise points of interest for me and which make me feel that there are dangers which should be recognised in the practice of TM. (Not that danger would ever dissuade me from praying or meditating.) On the semantic point may I make clear the Christian use of the word 'Meditation'. For me meditation involves conscious thought or concentration, whereas the prayer of simplicity (acquired contemplation) which I would parallel with TM as being close in kind, a simple mantra (aspiration), takes the subject away from conscious thought into a relaxed stillness. I find that often transcendental meditators misunderstand what we mean by 'contemplation'. For instance, Maharishi Mahesh Yogi says in his Commentary on the Bhagavad Gita. 'The process of contemplation and concentration both hold the mind on the conscious thinking level, whereas Transcendental Meditation systematically takes the mind to the source of thought, the pure field of creative intelligence.' Well, as one who has practised contemplative prayer for many years I know that contemplation does not hold the mind on any conscious level of thinking. Indeed one Christian has a great deal to say about this type of prayer in *The Cloud of Unknowing.* Forgive the digression. Anyway what I meant to bring out into the open is that so far a great deal of study is being done on the physiology of TM, and so far as we know no comparable studies have been done on Christians who contemplate.

A.C. No. But St Teresa's descriptions of some of the physiological effects of her mystical states sound very similar.

Questioner. But was she talking about the same state? She was in trance, whereas what you are talking about, and what Maharishi describes is what Christian writers on mystical development, notably Augustine Baker, call 'habitual acquired contemplation'. The Maharishi probably knows about the further stages they call 'infused contemplation', but TM is concerned with the former stage.

A.C. It is concerned with a natural state of stillness where something is allowed to happen; the organism seems to have an innate capacity to go into this state; and it is open to everyone.

J.W. You don't need to start from any particular religious beliefs. All you need in order to learn the technique is an intact nervous system, that is, simply one which is capable of thought. Changes in autonomic functioning occur effortlessly, automatically.

U.K. Will you remind me of the physiological effects of TM which as I understand it have now been widely studied, particularly by Wallace and Benson in America and Fenwick and Allison in England?*

A.C. Might we list these?

      Fall in oxygen consumption.

      Fall in respiratory rate.

      Slight fall in heart rate.

      Slight fall in blood pressure.

      Fall in blood lactate level.

      Increase in electrical skin resistance.

      A number of Electroencephalograph changes, including increased intensity of 'slow' alpha waves with occasional theta wave activity.

U.K. Am I right in thinking that the most significant changes are the E.E.G. changes and the blood lactate level response?

A.C. I should say that the most important change is the fall in metabolic rate, which is *not* associated with a loss of awareness.

J.W. I should emphasise that TM is effortless, and involves no control. The technique is a systematic way of producing the conditions in which the nervous system reacts on its own. Everything goes by itself. It could only be dangerous if effort was involved because this would

* See Wallace, "Wakeful hypometabolic physiological state", *American Journal of Physiology*, Vol. 221, No. 3, Sept 1971; J. F. Allison, *Lancet*, 1970, Vol. 1, 833–834; Wallace, "Physiology of meditation", *Scientific American*, Feb. 1972, Vol. 226, No. 2.

raise the possibility that the nervous system was being pushed in the wrong direction.

U.K. But there must be some 'work', in the technical physical sense of 'work', in the brain to alter an electro-encephalograph. Also if you alter the state of the autonomic nervous system, you alter the level of hormones in the hypothalamic part of the brain. This is where I see possible dangers, particularly with young persons. In young persons the autonomic nervous system is less stable, and they can get more easily into altered states of consciousness. Chemical alterations in the brain can alter their perception and they can get into difficulties over this. I think that before we interfere with the known mechanisms we have to have a lot more evidence about reversible and irreversible electro-chemical responses. For instance, we know that in the drug field we are able to suppress anxiety with phenothiazines and we can produce a comparable effect with more permanent results with modified leucotomies. In some way the arousal system is modified and I cannot hold that the results of that are always reversible when you remove the drug. The brain has a habit of doing its own internal biofeed-back technique. An illustration is the way in which an anxiety state can become chronic after a single episode provoking fear. The car crashes, the patient is afraid. There are chemical changes in the central nervous system. In some people the nervous system seems to develop its own feed-back system so that, although it is no longer stimulated externally, it goes on producing chemical changes resulting in anxiety.

J.W. When we speak of 'alteration' in the functioning

of nervous system we are referring to the temporary *reduction in activity* which occurs spontaneously during meditation. This is the precise opposite of 'work'. Its essence is deep rest during which physiological abnormalities (stresses) are automatically neutralised.

U.K. I still think we are still using the word 'work' in two different ways. You are describing lack of externally observable activities, I am saying that in order to produce rest, or any change whatever, 'work' in the physicist's sense of exchange of energy has to take place.

J.W. The restfulness – which physiologists have shown to be deeper than sleep – is proof of the effortlessness of the process. To cause damage it is necessary to make an effort of some sort. Among the indicators of the self-sufficiency of the state which occurs during TM is the fact that although oxygen consumption falls to about 20 per cent, there is no compensatory over-breathing afterwards. The state appears to be integrated because lower overall oxygen consumption co-exists with increased distribution of oxygen due to increased blood-flow, and brainwave patterns associated with both sleep and alertness occur simultaneously.

A.C. I would here remark that the long-term results seem to be invariably beneficial. I must emphasise that TM does not manipulate the nervous system in any way. On the contrary, during meditation one simply lets the attention take its own direction, which is in the direction of greatest attraction ('inwards'), and on the physical level this is accompanied by certain changes. But what is remarkable about this process is that all the physiological changes occur *spontaneously*. They could best be compared, perhaps, to the changes which occur during sleep. The TM state appears to be a 'fourth' *natural* state of the body, which complements and sustains the ordinary waking, dreaming, and deep sleep states. I would say that what is dangerous is *not* allowing this state to occur!

U.K. Do you really know that it is invariably beneficial? All teachers of TM haven't medical knowledge, so do they really know who should and who should not be encouraged to do it? You have to consider not only the teaching but the person to whom it should be given.

A.C. You would obviously need to give personal attention in the early stages of TM to people whom you found were disturbed, and advise them, for instance, to reduce the time they spent on it. There could be a danger if people go in for long periods of meditation without balancing them with normal activities. Maharishi emphasises the need for a balance of these two sides. And TM is meant for normal people, not as a therapy for severely disturbed people. The point is that we are not trying to produce altered states of consciousness but to allow the body to get rid of its stress.

U.K. What about the likeness and difference of the effects of TM and the effects of drugs? Zaehner has compared drug induced states with those described in the Upanishads, with the corollary that if drug-induced states are dangerous, so is TM, which is a method for

L

producing similar states. But he is surely wrong to claim
that drug-produced and manic states and these kind of
meditative states are similar. People in the drug scene
are wanting to go straight to the experiences, leaving out
the preparatory foundation which I take it Maharishi is
teaching.

A.C. As regards Zaehner's remarks about mysticism
and drugs, I hold that these have no application to TM.
I would not accept his claim that drug-induced states
and the states described in the Upanishads are identical
or even closely similar. I have discussed this question at
some length in my book *Seven States of Consciousness*;
it's a bit complicated to go into in detail here.

U.K. I would like to take you up on one point. You
have assumed that a release of stress is always beneficial.
I disagree. Have we any real evidence that it is a good
thing in apparently well people for their 'fight-flight' responses to be diminished? Aren't these mechanisms in fact
as natural as you claim the TM state to be, and do we
know what we are doing when we suspend normal
mechanisms which operate in people and which are known
physiological responses to stress?

J.W. Stress causes suffering and can't be good.

A.C. It certainly can't be good if it shows there is malfunctioning in the organism.

J.W. We are not suspending the normal mechanisms
which operate in people. TM *is* a normal mechanism.
As Anthony said, it must be balanced with activity.

And during activity meditators have been shown to cope better with stressful stimuli. The skin-resistance tests by Orme Johnson, which Una cites, did not indicate a diminution of the 'fight-flight' response of meditators. What they did show was their more rapid habituation to a given stressful stimulus – in this case a loud noise administered at irregular intervals. Initial reaction to it by meditators was just as lively as that by non-meditators, but meditators got used to it quicker – an appropriate response in this case because the sound, though disturbing, was not a real threat to their well-being. The conclusion must be that the 'fight-flight' response of meditators is not dulled but becomes more refined and more stable. They cope with stress more effectively.

U.K. I mentioned simple kinds of stress which can be reactions to danger. The use of stress can even be therapeutic. Some kinds of depression respond dramatically to a therapy in which the patient is deliberately kept awake all night. It is interesting to note that the depression doesn't always return with the passage of time. Something beneficial has happened as a result of prolonged wakefulness, though the system left to itself would naturally go to sleep. And there are even more important kinds of stress arising out of your relation to your environment, some of them because you have got to do something difficult, for instance learning something difficult. There is stress before playing a match, and you need both to feel it and surmount it. Even more before some public performance, and you won't perform so well without that kind of nervous tautness before you start.

Qu. Also one may be free from stress because one is coasting along and not dealing with problems in oneself and in one's relations with other people, and when one comes to go deeper into this, one will have to face stress.

A.C. We must distinguish 'challenge' from the environment, which is good, and 'stress' in the individual, which means malfunctioning and can only be bad.

You should get to a state of being able to function properly without stress. Even where there is still some stress, TM can prevent you from overreacting. For instance if you are startled by a motor horn suddenly sounding behind you, the effects pass off quickly. You don't go on feeling them, because there is less 'noise' in the system.

Qu. But sometimes stress is a condition for producing something. What about Beethoven when he produced his sonatas? It would not have been better for the world if he had been told he must get rid of stress.

A.C. But wouldn't it have been better for Beethoven?

Qu. Not if what he really wanted was to produce the sonatas. After all, what we want is a genius and sanctity, not just contentment. But there is another problem: you say that for the Maharishi liberation is a physiological matter.

A.C. Yes.

Qu. This is revealing. But this need not be the same as spiritual liberation.

A.C. I think it is.

U.K. Is a purely physiological release going to take you to the deepest levels? The use of a mantra can work in different ways at different levels. You say you are just giving people a technique for inner liberation, but you don't give them a way of dealing with their outer life. If it is a technique, there is the question of what it is to be used for; there is a responsibility on people who set something like this going to think about how it is to be used socially. It is said the American Government is prepared to have soldiers taught TM *en masse* to release tensions. But they are then going to be asked to do the very same thing that caused the tensions. There could be a cynical use of the meditation technique, if it is just taken as a technique on its own. I well believe the pace of our society is such that people need something like TM. Equally, there could be a selfish use of the technique, from hours spent engaged in meditative relaxation. Other traditions of meditation have said there must also be a moral side.

A.C. Other traditions have said: Become moral and then meditate. Maharishi says meditate and you will then become a moral person.

Qu. But if you are going to release tension, you have got to think about the social environment in which people are having to live. It can take them and use them for its purpose. Gary Snyder, in writing about Zen Buddhism says that Zen, like water, can flow into any mould. He thinks that it has good effects on Americans, who are individualistic and used to making moral protests. But with the Japanese, it will never encourage them to rise against any tyranny. The Japanese and Germans, when they take to Zen, already have all too much obedience in their bones. TM is now being poured into moulds of various cultures. We need a world-wide test to see whether it does something to people which wouldn't be expected from the culture. Will it, for instance, do something the American Army doesn't expect? Or can it be used in the service of any cause whatever?

J.W. If you wanted to manipulate people, you would need a technique which weakens them, whereas TM makes them stronger.

A.C. And the strength isn't independent of the moral aspect. The criminal, for instance, doesn't become a more effective criminal through TM.

Qu. But can it combine with *any* moral system?

A.C. Yes and no. Maharishi says moral activity consists in working in harmony with cosmic law, and meditation puts you in this harmony.

Qu. Some kinds of metaphysics – Schopenhauer's for instance, and Nietzsche's – would say cosmic law is quite ruthless and amoral. There is a real question here; also can you have it both ways? saying TM is only a technique, and then also making a metaphysical statement about it being in tune with the law of the cosmos?

J.W. I find no difficulty in combining these viewpoints. During the psycho-physiological procedures of TM, we spontaneously contact the unmanifest value of what Maharishi calls 'creative intelligence'. This pure intelligence, he teaches, functions at every level of creation. It is the basic nature of the mind, the basic nature of creation and the fundamental value of the process of evolution.

So, by regularly experiencing that basic value within us through TM, we create the conditions in which the manifest qualities of creative intelligence – its self-sufficiency, integration and progressiveness – spontaneously emerge in our everyday thought and activity. We ensure that our progress is upheld by the principles on which the entire progress of life is based.

U.K. One of the points I stressed in my article was hesitation about unleashing meditation from a considered way of life. You talk about alternating meditation and activity, but how much do you think about the kind of activity you alternate with? If you build a way of life into the use of the technique, then can the technique be used profitably by Christians, for instance, or Buddhists, in the setting of their own views?

A.C. Certainly, Maharishi tells people they should remain within their own religious traditions.

Qu. But every religious tradition has spoken of something which in Christian terms is called 'self-naughting'. Also in Christianity there is a process of becoming aware of one's pattern of faults and virtues, without fuss. This can take a long time to achieve – perhaps 20 years. How is the TM training going to connect with this?

A.C. You get an idea of renunciation during meditation, but it is renouncing of peripheral things, such as thinking about your failings and your wanting to be better. Dom John Chapman, a Christian writer on prayer, also said you must give these up.

U.K. You can give them up when you have learnt their shape. You are only allowing for one sort of person, not for the sort of person who needs to use his will and his wits in order to relate to the pattern of his deepest desires. And why shouldn't he?

A.C. Because then he would be setting up a partial view of what he ought to be.

U.K. You have a will and wits, and why shouldn't you have some say in the kind of skills and characteristics you want to develop? Pope John was this sort of person. He had many years in which he was thinking about his faults – his temper, for instance – as you can read in his *The Story of a Soul*, and he ended up a king of men.

J.W. If you want to improve yourself – and TM is one of many techniques for self improvement – then you should ensure that your activities in this direction are effective and unmistakable. TM accomplishes the goal most effectively because it spontaneously and directly produces more effective people. By spontaneously improving yourself you become better able to improve yourself! Meditators don't waste much time worrying about their shortcomings. They just meditate regularly and find that their behaviour naturally becomes more effective, more harmonious.

U.K. What do you say about the problem of evil? I meet it in myself, and not only in my ordinary mental experiences; I meet it when I go down into myself. How do you help people to cope with the difficulties they come up against when they are getting down to being more aware of themselves? They can be undoing their conditioning, and run into things – obsessions, rages – which had been buried. They can become aware of daemonic forces in themselves.

A.C. You get down to an absolute with bliss quality, where these things are transformed from below and become irrelevant.

U.K. But you have to go up and down and may not be very good at it. I am puzzled by your ignoring the journey.

A.C. The mantra is a means to take you down. It puts the body in a particular frame in which it is safe from these things.

Qu. I am not sure there is any state of absolute security from evil. Even at deep levels, something can go wrong, though pride for instance. Do you really reach a state where everything is absolutely O.K.? But your great strength is that you are prepared to make TM open to testing.

Qu. One interesting question would be whether other rhythmic activities – some kinds of manual work, or some kinds of physical exercise – have the same sort of results as TM is said to have.

J.W. They couldn't because TM isn't an activity, but a state of deep rest physiologically distinguishable from the everyday waking state during which physical exercise takes place.

Qu. This can be a question of words, since rhythmic repeating of a mantra is going on, and this is surely a kind of exercise. And the sort of breathing the Zen archer was taught to do was a very TM-like activity. Anyhow, if you are prepared to test for corresponding effects in people doing rhythmic work and exercise, look out! It might turn out that their blood lactate level was reduced.

A.C. I do not think we can decide the issue by arm-chair discussion. What we need are lots of long-term follow-up studies. Such studies are already being carried out in this country and elsewhere, and it will be much easier to talk about the question when we have more 'hard' information.

References

Chapter 1

1. Peggy Holroyde, et al, *East comes west*, Community Relations Commission Publications, p. 20.
2. Ibid, p. 23.
3. World Plan handout, 1972.
4. *Church of England Year Book*, C.I.O. (1973), p. 175.
5. John Windsor, *Guardian*, 19.1.73.
6. House Resolution No. 677, 77th General Assembly, House of Representatives, U.S.A.
7. A. Campbell, *Seven States of Consciousness*, V. Gollancz (1973), p. 30.

Chapter 2

1. K. N. Sen, *Hinduism*, Penguin (1961), p. 14.
2. Ibid, p. 21.
3. *Bhagavad Gita*, Tr. Juan Mascaro, Penguin (1962), ch. 12, vv. 13–14.
4. Ibid., ch. 12, vv. 6–8, p. 96.
5. Ibid., ch. 9, vv. 26–7. p. 82.
6. Maharishi Mahesh Yogi, *The Science of Being and Art of Living*, SRM (1963), p. 19.
7. Ibid., p. 32.
8. Ibid., pp. 33–4.
9. Ibid., p. 51.
10. Ibid., p. 61.
11. David Sykes, *Maryland Law Forum*, 1972.
12. Maharishi Mahesh Yogi, *Bhagavad Gita Commentary*, Penguin (1966), ch. 2, v. 51, p. 145.
13. Ibid., ch. 2, v. 56, p. 155.
14. Ibid., ch. 2, v. 57, p. 157.
15. Ibid., ch. 3, v. 58, p. 193.

16. *The Science of Being and Art of Living*, p. 276.
17. Ibid., p. 229.
18. Ibid., p. 228.
19. Ibid., p. 121.
20. Ibid., p. 82.

Chapter 3

1. Cyril Dunne, *Observer*, 14.1.68.
2. *The Science of Being and Art of Living*, p. 124.
3. Ibid., p. 170.
4. Maharishi Mahesh Yogi, *Bhagavad Gita Commentary*, Penguin (1966), ch. 3, v. 20, p. 214.
5. K. Wallace and M. Benson, A wakeful hypometabolic physiological state, *American J. Physiol.*, vol. 221, No. 3 (Sept. 1971), pp. 795–8.
6. Allison, Respiration changes during TM, *Lancet*, vol. 1 (1970), pp. 833–4.
7. P. Fenwick, Maudsley Institute, London.
8. Y. Sugi and K. Akutsu, Studies on respiration and metabolism during sitting in Zazen, *Res. J. Phys.*, Ed. 12, pp. 190–206 (1968).
9. B. K. Anand, G. S. Chinna and B. Singh, Historical survey of physiological studies in Zen, *E. E. G. Clin Neurophysiol.*, 13, pp. 452–6 (1961).
10. A. Campbell, *Seven States of Consciousness*, Gollancz (1973), p. 29.
11. N. Carroll, Today's Health, *J. Amer. Med. Association*, vol. 50, No. 4 (April 1972).
12. M. Benson and K. Wallace, Decreased drug abuse with TM, *Proceedings of International Conference* (1972). Ed. C. J. D. Zarafonatis, Philadelphia, Lea and Febiger, pp. 369–76.
13. W. T. Winquist, *The Effect of TM on students involved in the regular use of hallucinogenic and 'hard' drugs*, UCLA Sociology Dept. (1969). Available from MIU-Icsr.
14. Dr Leon Otis, *Stanford Research Unit* (1972). Quoted in John Windsor's article, *Guardian*, 19.1.73.
15. *The Science of Being and Art of Living*, p. 290.

Chapter 4

1. Holmes and Rahe, The social readjustment scale, *J. Psychosomatic research* (1967), vol. 11, pp. 213–18.

2. Rahe and Arthur, A longitudinal study of Life Change and illness patterns, *J. Psychosomatic research* (1967), vol. 10, pp. 355–66.

3. Alvin Toffler, *Future Shock*, Bodley Head (1972), p. 295.

4. Hugh Eadie, Psychological Health of Clergymen, *Contact*, No. 42 (Spring 1973), I.R.M.

5. H. B. Hale, E. W. Williams, et. al., *Aerospace Medicine* (1971), vol. 42, p. 127.

6. S. Cobb and R. M. Rose, *J. Amer. Med. Association* (1973), vol. 224, p. 489.

7. R. K. Smith, B. B. Cobb and W. E. Collins, *Aerospace Medicine* (1972), vol. 43, p. 1.

8. Decreased Blood pressure in hypertensive subjects who practised Meditation, Supplement 2, *Circulation*, vols. 45–6 (Oct. 1972).

9. E. F. Schumacher, *Small is beautiful*, Blond Briggs (1973).

Chapter 5

1. Jung. Quoted in *Mysticism* by F. C. Happold, Pelican (1963), p. 37.

2. W. James, *Varieties of Religious Experience*, Longmans (1902), p. 370 ff.

3. F. C. Happold, *Prayer and Meditation*, Pelican (1971), p. 93.

4. Dionysius the Areopagite, *Mystical Theology*.

5. Ruysbroek, *Seven degrees of love*. Quoted in *Mysticism* by F. C. Happold, p. 66.

6. *Dark night of the soul*, St John of the Cross, Bk. 2, ch. 17.

7. *Bhagavad Gita*. Tr. J. Mascaro, Penguin (1962), ch. 10, v. 23.

8. Job, chs 1–2.

9. Nicholas of Cusa, *The Vision of God*, ch. 9.

10. Galatians, 2:20.

11. Meister Eckhart. Quoted in *Mysticism* by F. C. Happold, p. 49.

12. St Teresa of Avila, *Interior Castle*, 7th mansion, ch. 2.

13. Blessed J. Ruysbroek, *Sparkling Stone*.

14. Julian of Norwich, *Revelations of Divine Love*, ch. 56. Grace Wartlock, Methuen, Sloan Mss.

15. 14th Century Unknown, *The Cloud of Unknowing*. Tr. C. Wolters, Penguin (1961), ch. 7.

16. *The Way of a Pilgrim*. Tr. R. M. French, Phillip Allen, p. 21.

17. Pseudo-Dionysius, *Mystical Theology*, ch. 2.

18. Dom Cuthbert Butler, *Western Mysticism*, Constable (1967 ed.), p. xlvii.
19. St Bernard, *Commentary on Song of Songs*. Quoted ibid., p. 101.
20. St Teresa of Avila, *Interior Castle*, 5th Mansion.
21. A. Bloom, *Living prayer*, Darton, Longman and Todd (1966), p. 93.
22. St Teresa of Avila, *Interior Castle*, 5th mansion.
23. Abishiktananda, *Prayer*, S.P.C.K. (1967), p. 43.
24. Père de Caussade, *Abandonment to Divine Providence*, Catholic Records Press, p. 136.
25. *The Way of a Pilgrim*. Tr. R. M. French, pp. 21, 22.
26. Abishiktananda, *Prayer*, S.P.C.K. (1967), p. 42.
27. Dom Aelred Graham, *Times* article, 23.12.73.
28. K. Leech, *Youthquake*, Sheldon Press (1973), p. 198.
29. R. D. Laing, *Politics of experience and Bird of Paradise*, Penguin, p. 114.

Chapter 6

1. Alison Peers, *Collected works St John of the Cross*, Burns Oates, vol. 2, p. 176.
2. Berrigan/Nhat Hahn, Contemplation and resistance, *Peace News*, 18.5.73, p. 5.
3. Romans 7:19–20.
4. Romans 7:21.

Chapter 7

1. T. Merton, *Contemplation in a world of action*, Allen and Unwin (1973), p. 212.

Selected list of books for further reading

Books by and about Maharishi Mahesh Yogi

1. Maharishi Mahesh Yogi, *The Science of Being and Art of Living*. SRM Publications, 1963.
2. Maharishi Mahesh Yogi, On the *Bhagavad Gita. Commentary*, Chapters 1–6 (new translation), Penguin, 1967.
3. Helena Olson, *A hermit in the house*. Available from SRM, 32 Cranbourn Street, London WC1.
4. Anthony Campbell, *Seven States of Consciousness*, Gollancz, 1973.

Books about Hinduism and other religions

1. K. M. Sen, *Hinduism*, Penguin, 1961.
2. Peggy Holroyde et al, *East comes West*, Community Relations Commission.
3. A. C. Bouquet, *Comparative Religions*, Penguin, 1941.
4. Herbert Slade, *Meeting schools of oriental meditation*, Lutterworth Education, 1973.
5. Juan Mascaro, *Bhagavad Gita*. (Translated from the Sanskrit with an introduction.) Penguin, 1962.

Books on Prayer and Mysticism

1. *Complete works of St Teresa of Avila*. Tr. Allison Peers. Sheed and Ward, 1972.
2. *Complete works of St John of the Cross*. Tr. Allison Peers. Sheed and Ward.
3. Julian of Norwich (Tr. Clifton Wolters), *Revelations of Divine Love*, Penguin, 1966.
4. Clifton Wolters, Translator of *The Cloud of Unknowing*, Penguin, 1961.
5. R. M. French, Translator of *The Way of a Pilgrim*, Philip Allan, 1930.

6. F. C. Happold, *Prayer and Meditation*, Pelican original, Penguin, 1971.
7. F. C. Happold, *Mysticism*, Penguin, 1963.
8. F. C. Happold, *The Journey Inwards*, Darton, Longman and Todd, 1966.
9. Anthony Bloom, *Living Prayer*, Darton, Longman and Todd, 1966.
10. Anthony Bloom, *School for Prayer*, Darton, Longman and Todd, 1970.
11. Abhishiktananda, *Prayer*, S.P.C.K., 1967.

Works of General Interest

1. William James, *The Varieties of Religious Experience*, Longmans, Green and Co., 1952.
2. Dom Cuthbert Butler, *Western Mysticism*, Constable, 1922. 3rd Ed. 1967.
3. Bede Griffiths, *Christian Ashram*, Darton, Longman and Todd, 1966.
4. Thomas Merton, *Contemplation in a World of Action*, Allen and Unwin, 1971.
5. Kenneth Leech, *Youthquake*, Sheldon Press, 1973.
6. Alvin Toffler, *Future Shock*, Bodley Head.